Measuring Software Quality

Richard Watts

PUBLISHED BY NCC PUBLICATIONS

British Library Cataloguing in Publication Data

Watts, Richard A.
Measuring software quality.
1. Computer programs — Evaluation.
I. Title
005.3 QA76.76.E93

ISBN 0-85012-557-X

First published in 1987 by:

NCC Publications, The National Computing Centre Limited, Oxford Road, Manchester M1 7ED, England.

Typeset in 10pt Times Roman by Impact Typesetting Manchester Limited, and printed by Hobbs the Printers of Southampton.

ISBN 0-85012-557-X

Preface

This book is based on the work of the MQ Project, which was carried out jointly by staff from GMD (Gesellschaft für Mathematik and Datenverarbeitung GmbH, Bonn, FRG) and NCC. This MQ project was part of the multi-annual research programme Specification and Development of Software Systems (SDSS) sponsored jointly by the Commission of the European Communities and the respective national governments.

We are grateful to have been given the opportunity to analyse the extent to which the need for objective means of software quality measurement and evaluation can be satisfied.

We have decided to publish this material in the form of a book, in the expectation that this will stimulate thought about quality matters. Any comments, criticism or suggestions will be received gratefully.

Acknowledgements

I would like to thank all those who have contributed to this work, especially Marie-Luise Christ, Harald Geist, Wolf Itzfeldt, Monika Schmidt and Michael Timm of GMD and David Law of NCC.

Contents

1 Introduction

1.1 MEASURING QUALITY

It is interesting to consider why it is now becoming more fashionable to measure the quality of software. There is more to this than mere fashion alone. As the data processing (DP) industry (today part of 'information technology') has matured, many inefficiencies in the production of software have been recognised. In particular the resultant systems have needed costly 'maintenance'. Also monolithic systems have been built which do not serve the real needs of users.

All this has led to a call for better quality software – so attention on what quality is and how it can be measured. There are in some cases legal obligations to provide 'quality' software, particularly where life and death (or large sums of money) are at stake, and there are very often economic advantages in producing products that are known to be good. The DP users too are subject to legal and economic constraints and find that they can better fulfil their operational functions with software of high quality.

There are two reasons for wanting to measure software quality:

- firstly predictive, in that the software producer needs to be able to know that what he is going to produce will perform its function to a high quality specification;
- secondly, after the software has been produced, potential users wish to know (a) that it meets their requirements and (b) how it compares with other software, if any, which might be used to carry out the same work.

In fact it is difficult to measure software quality to meet these requirements. You have to be sure that what you are measuring is an indicator of an actual quality characteristic, and one that it is useful to measure.

You also need to decide how important various characteristics are to you. This book will explain how software quality is a 'multidimensional' concept — that it has a number of individual characteristics which can each be evaluated or broken down into their constituent parts for lower-level investigation. It will therefore tell you about 'multidimensional' methods for amalgamating the results of measurements or evaluations.

Mostly this book will discuss measuring software quality, but it will also explore an approach to choosing development methods which will be of interest to many DP practitioners.

1.2 PURPOSE

The purpose of the research that went into the making of this book was to try to further the practice of measuring quality (perhaps to turn it from a 'black art' into a usable tool). In particular we hoped to discover whether there exist any objective means for software quality measurement and evaluation.

The work was in fact split up into a number of specific tasks which included:

- Seeing whether the definition of quality is generally agreed (it is easier to measure something where the ground is firm and not forever shifting);
- Seeing what measurement and evaluation techniques exist. With the means at our disposal we had to look mainly at the literature: we were unable to find many real world users. Part of the reason for publishing is to obtain more feedback about the techniques and facilities that might be in current use;
- Deciding what it means to say that a measure is 'good' (we also found it easier to compare measures after we had devised our own description scheme);
- Investigating the multidimensional methods which are needed to amalgamate the raw results of measurement, and devising a framework of instructions for the use of some of these;

- Using a questionnaire approach to the selection of software production aids. We concentrated on design methodologies (described later in the book) and are currently extending this scheme to look at requirements definition methodologies.

1.3 AN OVERVIEW OF THE BOOK

It is useful to indicate what the book covers. This will enable those with specific needs to go direct to the sections that concern them.

In Chapter 2, we discuss quality – how it can be considered as a collection of characteristics, each of which can be broken down into intermediate and lower-level attributes (product properties that can be measured). We also give an overview of measurement and evaluation.

From this we elaborate (in Chapter 3) the MQ model, developed by NCC and GMD and talk about what measures and measurement approaches are available. We discover many gaps in the coverage given by existing measures.

We look next (Chapter 4) at the possibilities of multidimensional software quality evaluation. This is needed where there are no valid measures and also for the amalgamation of the individual measured results onto a judgement scale which is meaningful for the characteristic as a whole.

We next explain (Chapter 5) the use of questionnaires for selecting development methodologies.

It is important that measures used should themselves satisfy certain criteria of goodness. We explain what these criteria are (Chapter 6) and outline a validation procedure which can be adopted.

Finally we draw conclusions, ask you to consider your own quality needs, and point at some areas where further research is needed. The conclusions are also summarised below (1.4): we would like to draw your attention to them before discussing the subject in detail.

1.4 CONCLUSIONS

Everyone should consider their own quality requirements and decide which are most important for them.

The quality model acts as a framework to hold the more detailed attributes and product properties. The level of detail can be broken down more and more (we do not claim here to be comprehensive).

Measurement is difficult. There are many areas where measures are not available; and even where they are, they are not always validated. We offer some tests which will help you to consider the worth of any measures you do or might use.

There are effective ways of amalgamating values of individual measurements or of combining the results of a number of evaluations into a single judgement. It is important to use the right sort of method.

The approach to selecting methodologies is worth further development. It would take less effort on the part of the selector if there were answers readily available for those questions to which the answer is common. Obviously the user requirements will differ, but the scope of the methodologies should be much more static.

We would like to see more research on measures that really work. Such information would be of wide interest. To this end, as mentioned in the Preface, it would help us to know what statistics you currently keep. Do you in fact do so with quality in mind? Or do you use them to control productivity, or just because it seemed a good idea at the time?

2 Quality Characteristics

2.1 THE CONCEPT OF SOFTWARE QUALITY

There are two possible interpretations of the concept of software quality. Firstly, quality could be taken to mean the *degree of excellence*. This would however suppose that there is general agreement on the characteristics which are considered desirable and necessary (and the reverse) and also on the extent to which specific characteristics have to be present in order to fulfil general quality standards. Since it seems to us that there can be no such general agreement, we reject this interpretation of quality.

According to the second interpretation, quality is to be understood as the *degree of compliance* (or non-compliance) with specified requirements. Quality requirements are statements on characteristics of a software product (for example, on its maintainability) and on the desired extent of these characteristics for the type of use intended. The question is not "Which characteristics must a good product possess?" but rather "By which characteristics would a product be suitable for type of use X?" and "To what extent is a given product suitable for that type of use?"

We need then a conceptual framework which will help people to understand what quality is (in their own environment) and this is what is contained in Sections 2.2 and 2.3. We then (in Section 2.4) suggest some approaches which will allow them to apply this concept of quality to their own problems

2.2 OUR CONCEPTUAL FRAMEWORK

Quality manifests itself in a variety of characteristics: these and the relations between them depend on the context. We can begin by offering a set of quality characteristics which seem to cover all the important areas of software production. In fact what we have done is to develop one of the two most sophisticated decompositions of quality which have been published, that of McCall et al, 1977, (Figure 2.1) (Note: the other model is that of Boehm et al, 1978. There is a great deal of overlapping between these two).

We chose the one which appealed to us more, probably because it breaks each characteristic into a larger set of attributes (or criteria) which are shared between the characteristics in an interesting way. It is not a simple tree structure where each characteristic is broken down into a number of attributes, but in fact some attributes must be included in a number of characteristics. Having decomposed quality thus far, it is possible to specify – in a further step – 'operable' properties of the software that are likely to be easier to measure.

The other interesting aspect of the model is its division into three classes according to use, namely product operation, product revision and product transition; it will be interesting to see in due course (Section 2.3) how use affects the characteristics which need to be considered.

There has been much research into the breakdown of attributes into descriptive product properties, but it is often not clear to what extent such properties actually depict the quality attribute in question (and hence eventually the characteristic). We will continually come across this problem and indeed we explore it more fully in Section 2.6, where we examine what we mean by 'goodness' in a measure and also produce some validation procedures for measures.

We explore (in Section 2.3) some measures for individual properties and attributes which have been suggested and examined by researchers in this field. First it is useful to look at the problem of interdependency between different characteristics.

2.3 INTERDEPENDENCY

There are three different types of interrelations which can be distinguished.

Indifferent: in this case the extent of one characteristic (or attribute) has no effect on the extent of another.

Competitive: two quality characteristics are competitive when the increase of one of them entails a decrease in the other (and vice versa).

Complementary: here the increase of one quality characteristic is accompanied by the increase of another (and vice versa). In this case, one is not saying that the one *causes* the other, merely that the two effects always appear together.

The importance of establishing these interrelationships is to ensure that we are measuring the right thing. It would also be helpful to ensure that one could increase one desirable quality and at the same time help to achieve the conditions which give rise to a second quality. For example (looking again at Figure 2.1), it would appear that greater simplicity (as an attribute) may well give rise to greater reliability, maintainability and testability: but this does not necessarily mean that a maintainable program will also be testable. We would need to go further and show the value of the contribution that simplicity makes to each of the characteristics. In the long term, we would hope to discover the product properties which were the most valuable (in given circumstances). We are not yet in such a fortunate position and so must look more closely at the quality characteristics to see how they can be defined and what measures have been proposed.

2.4 QUALITY MEASUREMENT

Having decomposed quality into use, characteristics, attributes and properties, we need to go beyond the concepts themselves and to discover 'operational specifications'. What this means is that we have to find measures which are suitable: it is the type of property which determines the specific type of measurement which can be used. (Please note that throughout this section we have used only the word 'property', even though it may be that one is attempting to measure or evaluate a higher-level attribute or characteristic directly.)

2.4.1 Properties

There are four distinct types of properties:

Classificatory (nominal) properties whose degrees are determined by assignment to different classes; for example, the programming language used. Each such nominal property characterises an object by the possession of specific, exclusive sub-properties.

USE	CHARACTERISTIC	ATTRIBUTE
Product operation	Usability	Operability Training/familiarisation Communicativeness I/O volume and rate Data commonality
	Security (integrity)	Control and audit of access Integrity of data, etc
	Efficiency	Storage efficiency Execution efficiency
	Correctness	Completeness Traceability Consistency
	Reliability	Accuracy Error tolerance Simplicity Consistency
Product revision	Maintainability	Consistency Simplicity Conciseness Self-descriptiveness Modularity
	Testability	Simplicity Instrumentation Self-descriptiveness Modularity
	Flexibility	Expandability Generality Self-descriptiveness Modularity
Product transition	Re-usability	Generality Self-descriptiveness Modularity Machine independence Software system independence
	Portability	Self-descriptiveness Modularity Machine independence Software system independence
	Interoperability	Modularity Communications commonality Data commonality

(based on the GE Model by McCall et al, 1977)

Figure 2.1 The MQ Quality Model

Comparative (ordinal) properties whose degrees are determined by assignment to categories; for example, the degree of complexity of a module may be called low, medium or high. Ordinal properties allow us to rank or grade objects according to the extent to which they possess the given property.

Discrete properties whose degrees are determined by integers; for example, lines of code.

Continuous properties whose degrees are determined on a continuous scale by real numbers; for example, one might have a measure for a program which calculated its percentage efficiency.

The first two of these are often called 'qualitative' properties, the last two 'quantitative'.

2.4.2 Types of Scale

The results of measuring are transferred to the appropriate type of scale, and this determines the sort of mathematical transformation which can be used on the results. There are four types of scale:

Nominal scale: This is the scale suitable for classificatory properties. This is really the most primitive form of measuring (or evaluation). Permissible operations are counting and percent processes, and one may also take simple frequency statistics.

Ordinal scale: This constitutes the next higher measurement level and is to be used for comparative properties. The intervals between successive points on the scale are not known and by definition may not be of equal size. One may use statistical transformations which maintain the same rank order of the measuring results. Statistics available from ordinal scales are median, percentile and rank correlation coefficients; non-parametric tests like rank tests are also permissible.

Interval scale: Unlike the previous scales this is a quantitative scale which allows us to determine the degree of discrete properties. The units on the scale have equal intervals. Accordingly almost all mathematical (statistical) operations except the formation of quotients can be performed on the measuring results. The formation of expectation values and standard deviations is admissible as are product-moment correlations and all common parametric significance tests (t-tests and F-tests).

Ratio scale: This scale is the one which is suitable for measuring any continuous property. It has an absolute zero in addition to the interval scale so that the formation of quotients is also admissible. The scale is in fact in exactly the same ratio as the property being measured.

2.4.3 Quality Measures

What is being attempted in the field of software quality is the development of concepts that have been used in other quality fields for a considerable time. There has been much recent increased effort in the field of 'software metrics' by such workers as Gilb (1987), McCall (1980) and Perlis et al (1981).

We would like to define now what it means for a measure to be considered a 'good' quality measure.

A quality measure must:

- provide the connection between the quality characteristic (or attribute) and the product properties constituting that characteristic;
- react sensitively to different degrees of the quality characteristic to be measured;
- guarantee that it will provide objective determination of the quality characteristic and of the mapping of the results onto a suitable judgement scale.

There appear to be seven criteria of 'goodness' which quality measures have to meet (this subject is explored more fully in Chapter 6):

Objectivity: the measuring results obtained must be free from any subjective influences. It must not matter who the measurer is.

Reliability: a quality measure should secure stable and precise results however often the tests are carried out (assuming the conditions are comparable).

Validity: it is no use carrying out the test unless the measure really measures the correct characteristic.

Standardisation: there has to be a scale for unambiguous representation and comparison of the results.

Comparability: we need to know enough about the measure to allow us to compare it with other measures which claim to measure the same characteristic.

Economy: it is obviously desirable that the determination and evaluation of measuring values should involve as low cost as possible. This is obviously a matter of judgement: how does one ever determine how much quality is worth? All in all a simpler (cheaper) measure (even if it is slightly less accurate) is more likely to be used than a complicated (expensive) one.

Usefulness: a quality measure must satisfy a practical need. We add this rider to attempt to prevent people from measuring things which *can* be measured even though the results are not important to them.

2.5 EVALUATION OF QUALITY CHARACTERISTICS

The term 'evaluation' is used with two meanings. The context should indicate which is intended.

Firstly, it is used in the sense of allotting scores to characteristics for which there are no quantitative measures (as with the classificatory and comparative characteristics discussed above).

Secondly, it is used in the sense of a qualitative analysis following the use of one or more measures. This is a necessary step, because it is not valid to say that a particular score with a given measure is enough to satisfy the quality requirement of any evaluator. A measurement scale has to be mapped onto a subjective judgement scale.

Even if it is considered that a single measured property is enough to provide a reliable and objective measure of the quality characteristic and having put the degrees of the quality characteristic onto the judgement scale, there remains the problem of combining such judgement scales into a single combined evaluation of the quality of the product as a whole.

Although we offer (in Chapter 4) a number of multidimensional methods to help the evaluator with this problem, there are dangers of over-interpreting and of combining individual measured values in a numerically correct but logically meaningless manner.

For example, if the usability of two objects A and B were being compared on an ordinal scale from 1 to 5, it would be over-interpretation to say that object A was twice as usable as object B just because A was rated 4 and B was 2. There is no such relation as 'twice as great' on an ordinal scale.

An example is given by de Millo and Lipton (Perlis et al, 1981), of an estimating formula for the effort required for program development:

$$E = 2.7a + 121b + 26c + 12d + 22e - 497$$

where:

E = development effort (man-months)

a = estimated no. of statements/1000

b = complexity (subjective (1-5))

c = number of external documents

d = number of internal documents

e = size of database (in 'words')

The problem with such a formula is that it contains quantities of quite different dimensions and types of measurement. Consider, for instance, the meaninglessness of adding a program length and a complexity number; there is no logical connection. One can only carry out reasonable transformations.

Figure 2.2 gives a simplified view of the whole process of decomposition (to product features), measurement, evaluation and amalgamation. In principle there are two ways of combining measures for individual product properties to indicators of quality characteristics:

- If each product property can be assumed to be of equal relevance to the quality characteristic, the scores of the product properties can be added, but such a process ignores dependencies between individual product properties. (Examples of interdependency are the polarity profile and simple scoring methods described in Chapter 4).
- In order to take into account differential influences of a particular product, it is necessary to use a weighted summation formula. The weights may be determined by expert judgement or by experience. A number of examples of such formulae are given (also in Chapter 4).

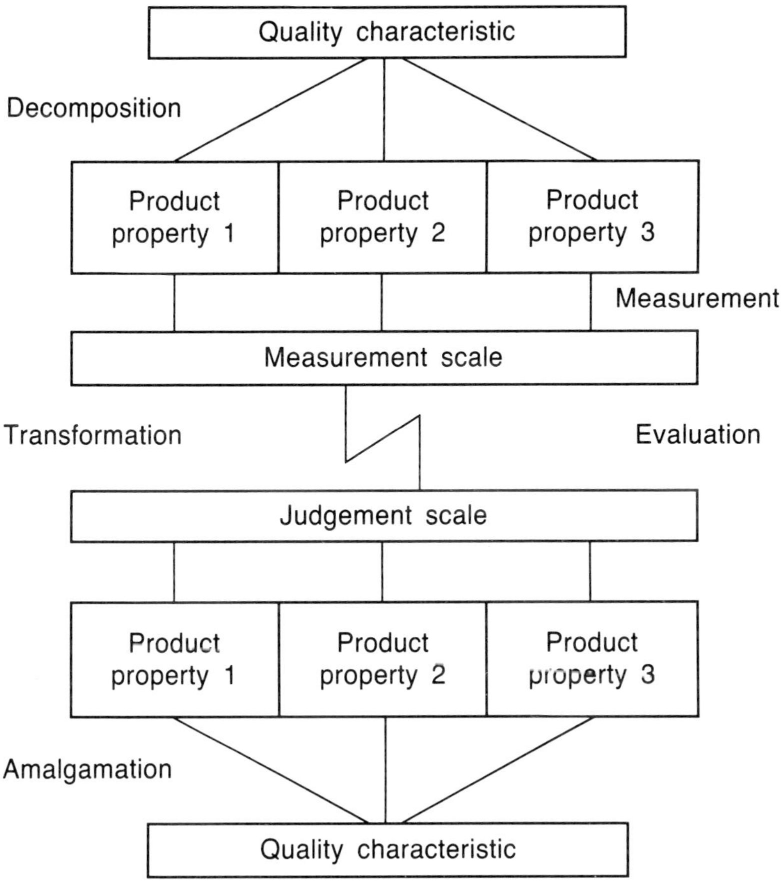

Figure 2.2 Measurement and Evaluation of a Software Quality Characteristic

3 The MQ Model: Measurement Approaches

3.1 THE GE MODEL AGAIN

Figure 2.1 showed a decomposition of the concept of 'quality'. In this chapter each of the characteristics will be described more fully and possible measurement approaches will be discussed.

The first thing to notice is that available measures are not evenly spread across the range of characteristics. Of 40 measures studied, (Table 3.1) the majority fall under only two headings — 18 under 'Maintainability' and 12 under 'Reliability'. This is partly because publication of one measure spurs the development of other variants — this is what appears to have happened with Halstead's 'software science' measures — and partly that reliability and maintainability have been areas of particular concern.

This uneven spread means that in order to evaluate quality overall, it is necessary to make use of the multidimensional methods described in Chapter 4. Even then the measures discussed only cover parts of the areas of reliability and maintainability.

It is best to let the measurement approaches speak for themselves. The measures themselves are further described in *Comparative descriptions of software quality measures* by Hoecker et al (1984) but reference to the original sources can be found in Appendix 1, which gives a brief supplementary description of each measure.

3.2 PRODUCT OPERATION

For the operation of a software product, it is vital that its handling is easy to learn, that it can be operated efficiently and effectively and that

Primary objectives and titles of measures	Secondary objectives
Usability	
Flesch-Kincaid Readability Index	
Fog Index	
Keystroke-Level Model	
Maier's Measure of User Friendliness	
Integrity	
Svans' Integrity Metrics	
Efficiency	
None (see text)	
Correctness	
Error Prediction Measure	Maintainability
Model of Defect Removal	
Pimont-Rault's Testing Measure	(see also Maintainability)
Reliability	
Complexity Measure based on Selection and Nesting	Correctness, Maintainability
Gilb's Logical Complexity Measure	Correctness, Maintainability
Knot Count Complexity Measure	Correctness, Maintainability
Minimal Intersection Number	Correctness, Maintainability
Myers' Interval Complexity Measure	Correctness, Maintainability
Thayer's Logic Complexity Measure	Maintainability
2-Tuple Complexity Measure	Correctness, Maintainability
Execution Time Measure	
Nelson's Reliability Measure	Correctness
Numerical Reliability Index	Correctness
Schick/Wolverton's Probabilistic Measure	
Littlewood's Measure of Availability	Usability
Maintainability	
De Young/Kampen's Readability Measure	Adaptability, Expandability
Gordon's Program Clarity Measure	Adaptability, Expandability
Joergensen's Readability Measure	Adaptability, Expandability
Halstead's Measure E	Adaptability, Expandability
McCabe's Cyclomatic Number	Correctness, Reliability
McClure's Complexity Measure	
Oveido's Program Complexity Measure	
Yin/Winchester's Measure of Software Design Quality	
Zolnowski/Simmons' Complexity Measure	Adaptability, Expandability
Logical Stability Measure	Adaptability, Expandability
Gilb's Structural Complexity Measure	Reliability, Interoperability
Keutgen's Measure of Intramodular Structure	Adaptability, Expandability
Myers' Module Independence Measure	Interoperability
Mohanty/Adamowicz's Test Measure	
Paige's Test Effort Measure	
Pimont/Rault's Testing Measure	(see also Correctness)
Test Effectiveness Metric	Correctness
Yin's Independence Metric	Correctness
Adaptability	
None (see under Maintainability)	
Expandability	
Maekawa's Measure of Extensibility	
Interoperability	
None (see under Maintainability)	
Re-usability	
None (see text)	
Portability	
Gilb's Portability Measure	

Table 3.1 List of Measures

both input and output are suited to the problems of the user. Our model includes all these aspects under the concept of usability. Further quality characteristics are *efficiency of execution,* including both use of storage capacity and run time, and *security,* which covers both integrity of data access and consideration of the problems of corruption of data and programs. The product must also be *correct,* in such a way that it must fulfil the required functions completely and in a traceable and testable manner.

Because it is difficult to prove correctness, *reliability,* which shows itself in continued accuracy of results, fault-tolerance, consistency and simplicity, must also be considered.

It should be stressed again that we are seeking ways to evaluate and measure these quality characteristics. Guidelines for the improvement of quality can be found in: *Quality assurance and control* (GMD and NCC, 1984); *Software validation: techniques and methods* (Abbott, 1984); and in *Software test aids* (Abbott, 1985).

3.2.1 Usability

Although much has been written on user friendliness (there are many guides to dialogue design (eg Watts, 1984) and discussions on the factors influencing usability), there are very few measures which would be helpful for either predictive or comparative evaluation of usability factors.

There is general agreement that one needs sufficient introductory material and information such as comprehensible error messages, recovery notification and HELP-functions. Usability can be measured by the average effort required for learning, operating and analysing the results.

It is now recognised that the user's needs are most important; thus measurement of effort alone is not enough. It has been shown, for instance, that it is possible to make the use of programs too simple for anyone but the most naive user. Thus Maier (1983), in his 'Measure of user friendliness' measures both ease of use and user satisfaction.

One measure which can be used for the prediction of usability in terms of the time a trained user will require for accomplishing a specific task is Card's 'Keystroke-level model' (1980).

Measures for text comprehensibility have also been studied, since the availability and ease of understanding of manuals and specifications is likely to have a strong effect on the quality of the software as a whole.

There are three approaches worth mentioning:

- syllable-type formulae;
- stored-vocabulary formulae;
- Text Impression Ratio.

In *syllable-type formulae,* word difficulty is defined by word length and sentence length. Examples are:

The *'Fog Index'* developed by Gunning (1968):

F = 0.4 × (sentence length (words) + percentage of words of three or more syllables)

The *Flesch-Kincaid 'Readability Formula'* is similar (Kincaid et al, 1981):

Grade level = 0.39 × sentence length (words) + 11.8 × word length (average no. of syllables per 100 words) – 15.59

Stored-vocabulary formulae rely on a vocabulary of common words. The disadvantages are that the vocabularies need to be compiled and maintained and manual computation is very difficult to achieve.

Text Impression Ratio has been developed at Hamburg University. It is a more qualitative approach to text comprehensibility, since it relies on the impression a text leaves on a group of trained readers, whose scores are combined to give an overall rating. The main disadvantage appears to be in the cost of developing and maintaining sufficient expertise to carry out such evaluations.

Preferred, therefore, is the simple syllable-type formulae which can either be calculated manually or automatically. It may be that such text analysis systems as the 'Computer Readability Editing System' or the 'Unix Writer's Workbench' will become more generally available to help writers achieve acceptable levels of readability.

3.2.2 Integrity

There are two senses in which integrity or security are required.

Firstly, the data or program needs to be protected against access by non-authorised persons, and, secondly, the environment (ie other programs and data) needs to be protected against the program.

In *Software safety,* Leveson (1982) considers the consequence of program errors for the environmental system and the users. Security relates to the avoidance of safety failures, particularly those leading to casualties or serious consequences. There is clearly a strong link here between integrity and reliability where we will again come across the problems of fault avoidance and fault removal.

In general this is not otherwise an area in which measurement has been carried out, though Svanks (1981) defines a number of characteristics and measures for quantifying the integrity of user-specific datasets. Relevant techniques of statistical quality control are also discussed in that paper.

3.2.3 Efficiency

Efficiency can be divided into:

- *execution efficiency* for which the reduction in processing time is the prime objective;
- *storage efficiency* for which the use of the minimum amount of storage, both internal and external is important.

It is often necessary to trade off one of these aspects against the other, but such resource management problems are outside the scope of this book. There are indeed no measures as such in resource management: it can be a matter of tuning the exact mix of processing on the given installation to which general rules cannot be applied.

Benchmark tests have been used in the assessment of implementation efficiency. Although they allow efficiency comparisons to be made under carefully controlled test conditions, problems are encountered in proving whether the benchmarks are representative.

It is fortunate for the data processing practitioner that hardware costs have fallen so dramatically over the years. This has meant that there has been less pressure for efficiency at the expense of other factors such as reliability, usability, etc. For this reason, very few measures exist specifically for efficiency as it affects quality evaluation.

3.2.4 Correctness

If correctness of software is to be understood as the extent to which a program complies with its specifications and fulfils the requirements of its users, a correct program can only be as good as its specifications and requirements. We should also consider the following three criteria:

- *completeness*, whereby the program provides the complete implementation of the required functions;
- *consistency,* whereby the software uses uniform design and implementation techniques and notations;
- *traceability,* in that there must be provided means of following up the requirements in the software as implemented.

Two approaches to evaluating the correctness of a program are worth distinguishing.

First, in the approach of Halstead (1977) the number of operators and operands of a program are regarded as measurable basic quantities. Formulae are developed which are said to give a general relationship between these and other elements of a program such as its 'volume' or the effort required to produce it. Halstead's Software Science Effort measure is also relevant to Maintainability (3.3.1).

Its relevance to correctness is that it is claimed that there is a high correlation between the published number of errors for a specific product and the 'Software Science Measure E' (total number of elementary mental discriminations) (Funami and Halstead, 1975). Ottenstein has developed formulae for assessing the number of errors in a program on acceptance testing (Ottenstein's Error Prediction Measure, 1979 and 1981).

The strongest objection is that it seems strange that the number of errors should depend only on the features of the program and not on the capabilities and work conditions of the developers. It may be that such formulae do in fact supply satisfactory estimates for a fairly homogeneous development team under nearly constant working conditions. Probably the parameters could be redefined to consider the peculiar conditions of the organisation but we are not aware that this has been done.

The second approach to evaluating correctness analyses the error detection process during the testing and integration phases of system development. From the number of detected errors the number of errors still contained in the system is deduced.

Remus and Zilles (1979) in their 'Model of Defect Removal' have developed a theory of how to use measurable quantities arising from the software development process, including the number of errors detected by reviews and tests, in assessing the effectiveness of the error analysis and detection process and the total number of errors. The theory rests on a number of assumptions, eg that the number of errors depends on the size of the program. Given sufficient data from a given installation, the validity of these assumptions could be tested.

Other possibilities which have been suggested for improving correctness include 'error seeding' (debugging and mutation analysis) whereby errors are inserted into the program or specific mutations are performed and all previous test cases are re-applied. It is the aim, after detecting inserted errors or non-equivalent mutations and then calculating the ratio of detected to undetected inserted errors, to estimate the number of undetected real errors.

3.2.5 Reliability

For many installations, the only reliability statistics kept are those on hardware availability – eg 'less than 3% down time' or '98.5% available' – which take no account of software behaviour at all.

Software reliability can be defined as the degree to which the software is fault-free.

A software failure will occur when the following three factors coincide:

- the software contains a fault;
- the data is such that when processed by the faulty part of the software, it will cause a processing error;
- the software contains no error-recovery algorithms able to cope with that particular error.

Since it is impossible to predict exactly when this coincidence will occur, the software failure time is random. It follows that software reliability can be defined in the same manner as the reliability of physical devices, that is as the probability that it will operate without failure within a given environment during a given interval of time.

We may therefore attempt to assess software reliability by measurement, estimation or prediction.

Measurement is the derivation of values for a reliability parameter of a program (eg the mean time to failure (MTTF) or failure rate) from failure data obtained by running the program in its normal environment.

Estimation is the derivation of similar values obtained by running the program in a different environment, such as during program testing.

Prediction involves the derivation of values by studying the properties of the software product as well as those of the software development process. It is therefore only possible if there is a thorough understanding of the factors which cause software failure.

Any estimated or predicted values of reliability parameters should be compared as soon as possible with those obtained by measurement.

By measuring the actual failure rate, we can also find the MTTF. After the software has passed its initial development debugging phase, a constant failure rate is often assumed though it is more likely that, as the number of residual faults changes, the failure rate will also change: it may decrease at each fault repair to model the improvement in software reliability in the early stages of its use; or it may increase to reflect the decrease in software reliability often observed to occur due to 'excessive' correction of the program.

There have been several models proposed for reliability estimation, but there does not seem to be any general agreement that any of them is sufficiently accurate. We suggest, however, that a cost-effective solution will be obtained by using one of the leading models and comparing the results obtained with actual measurements.

There is no method available for accurate prediction. In our view those attempts which have been made, based on complexity, by Halstead and others (as already discussed under 'Correctness' in 3.2.4) fail because they do not take any account of the development process. This is an area in which further research would be profitable: it would be helpful to know the relationship between residual faults and:

- complexity of software;
- ambiguity of software documentation;
- task complexity;
- environmental factors;
- quality of tools; and
- knowledge, skills and attitude of personnel.

Reliability Models

The models which have been proposed for reliability estimation can be divided into:

- class 1 models, which are based on the assumption that the software failure rate is proportional to the number of residual faults;
- class 2 models, which are not based on this assumption.

The criteria which should be applied to these models are:

- predictive validity;
- usefulness;
- quality of assumptions;
- applicability;
- simplicity.

Predictive validity is the capability of the model to predict future failure behaviour based on past and present failures.

Usefulness is assessed in terms of the facilities that the model offers for planning and controlling software development (and maintenance) activities. The model should provide therefore:

- present MTTF;
- likely date of reaching a specified MTTF;
- resources required.

Quality of assumptions is to be assessed by:

- the degree to which they are supported by actual data;

- their plausibility: are they logically consistent and in agreement with software engineering practice;
- their clarity: can they enable the area of applicability to be judged.

Applicability is assessed in terms of:

- the range of software to which the model is applicable;
- compatability with hardware models;
- the variety of situations to which the model can be applied, eg classification of severity of failures and use at design changes.

Simplicity should be considered in terms of:

- the data;
- the concepts from which the model is constructed;
- the relationship of parameters used by the model to physical properties of software;
- the capabililty for implementation as a program that is easy to run.

(These criteria are taken from a joint paper by Iannino et al, 1983).

Having applied these criteria to the Musa 'Execution Time' model (Musa, 1975, 1979 and 1980)(Class 1) and to the Littlewood and Verall 'Bayseian' model (Littlewood, 1973 and 1974) (Class 2) we believe that the former is better because:

- it appears to be based on assumptions closer to the way in which most software engineers conceptualise the failure process, ie that failure is proportional to the number of residual faults;
- it appears to be more useful for project management purposes. It is certainly easier to understand and apply;
- it performs well on real-life data.

Musa's Execution Time Measure

The 'execution time' theory consists of the execution time component and the calendar time component, and is based on assumptions that appear to be met reasonably well by most executable programs and development projects, where testing is representative of the operational environment and failures are observed. Musa has derived a number of equations relating failures experienced, present MTTF, cumulative execution time, objective MTTF, failures to reach the MTTF objective established for the product, and the execution and calendar times estimated to reach this objective.

The measured quantities are the cumulative execution time (r), the total number of failures possible during the maintained life of the software (Mo) and the MTTF at the start of the test (To) defined as the expected value of the failure interval.

The method is to determine these three measured values. To estimate the testing compression factor C, it is normal to start from the conservative assumption that C is equal to 1 until experience proves otherwise.

Then the present MTTF (T) is calculated according to the formula:

$$T = To \exp (Cr/Mo.To)$$

and finally the length of the operational phase (r') is determined and the reliability (R) is calculated:

$$R = \exp (-r'/T)$$

A Fortran program has been developed to estimate the total failure expected during the maintained life of the software and the MTTF at the start of the test. This program requires as input the execution time intervals between failures experienced, the MTTF objective and the test environment factor.

Reliability improvement

In practical terms it will be of little use establishing what the current reliability factor is, unless it is also known how to improve that reliability if it is thought to be unsatisfactory. The three strategies which may be employed for such an improvement are:

- fault avoidance;
- fault removal;
- fault tolerance.

Traditionally the reliability of software was achieved largely by fault removal through testing and debugging. It was found that this was not effective enough. For high reliability, properly co-ordinated application of all three approaches is required.

Fault avoidance is based on the realisation that the most economical way of achieving reliability is to avoid the occurrence of human errors, which also has the economic advantage of reducing maintenance time. It seems that the most hopeful approach lies in imposing constraints on the process of software development to control the factors which cause people to make mistakes.

Fault removal can be made more effective by:

- checking for correctness at every stage;
- proving correctness against formal specifications;
- simulation of overall information system behaviour (eg prototyping);
- testing of implemented programs.

The inclusion of independent validators in the check for correctness after each task will often prove particularly effective.

Fault tolerance is a particular requirement of very complex software systems with very high reliability requirements and is based on the principle of redundancy coupled with error detection and error-recovery algorithms (Hecht, 1979 and Rzevski, 1980).

3.3 PRODUCT REVISION

It is generally recognised that product revision and maintenance, ie error correction, adaptation and expansion, use up a major part of the costs incurred by a system. Indeed in many organisations far too many resources are tied up in old systems. It is therefore very important that the quality characteristics which are associated should be measured or otherwise evaluated wherever possible.

Rather than the GE characteristics of maintainability, testability and flexibility, we prefer to call the characteristics directly after the three activity groups, error repair, adaptation and expansion, ie maintainability, adaptability and expandability.

3.3.1 Maintainability

In considering maintainability as that software characteristic which has an influence on error repair, we have to look for means of quantifying, measuring and evaluating the mean effort required for error detection and correction. We will discuss two approaches: the first tries to identify a minimum number of measurable properties which have a high correlation with observed maintenance behaviour; the second attempts a more comprehensive decomposition of sub-characteristics.

The Indicator Approach

By looking for indicators which have a high correlation with the characteristics of maintenance, it is hoped to get values which are helpful in the prediction of the future effort required for maintenance. Thus, Feuer and Fowlkes (1979) have studied in two papers the effect on error numbers per module and the time required to repair a single error of the following program properties:

- complexity of program flow;
- nesting structure of program flow;
- 'software science' values, such as program size, program level and decision density;
- localisation of variables.

They report the following results:

- most measured values are strongly dependent on the number of statements in the program.
- program size has proved to be a good indicator of maintenance behaviour (that is, of error density and error repair time). The increase in repair time with program size is linear with errors that are simple to repair, and appears to be exponential with those that are difficult to repair.
- if the influence of program length is computationally eliminated from the measured quantities, transformed measured quantities are obtained, among which the program level and decision density are of the greatest importance.

Both error density and number of modifications appear to be inversely proportional to the transformed program level, so for two programs of equal size it is the one with the lower level which shows the greater number of errors and modifications. For larger programs (defined as those with more than 60 edges) error density is directly proportional to decision density.

Further investigations pursuing this indicator approach are discribed by Sheppard (1979) and Krten and Levy (1980). This approach could also be related to 'complexity', in which, however, the link with error repair is not directly measured. Obviously if one can find such a direct link it will have great influence on the practicality of such measures for the DP practitioner and we would welcome further research in this direction; there is a particular need for statistics from more installations.

The Decomposition Approach

In this approach, we look in more detail at maintainability to try to identify the cause/effect relationship between product property and quality characteristic. Thus maintainability can itself be decomposed into sub-characteristics.

We will discuss the sub-characteristics analysability, modifiability and testability and their relationship with various product properties.

Analysability – there are two influential groups of software properties which need to be distinguished when looking for those allowing or facilitating error detection; the logical and linguistic difficulty.

We will discuss the logical difficulty, concerning the complexity of the control and data flows, under the heading 'testability' in accordance with most research. It is nevertheless clearly relevant both to the detection and correction of errors.

We need to consider the linguistic difficulty since, for successful maintenance, the program should be able to be read and understood. The following properties of comprehensibility are suggested:

- structuredness: the extent to which a program contains a previously defined pattern of organisation of its interdependent parts; that is, the program agrees with a specification that is itself comprehensive;
- self descriptiveness: the extent to which a program contains for the reader sufficient information about program objectives, assumptions, constraints, input/output, individual components

and status. There has long been an argument about how far the code should be self-contained on the grounds that the code is more likely to be kept up to date than the specification; but at the very least references to the specification are essential;

- consistency: the extent to which a program contains uniform notation, terminology and symbology. This becomes more of a problem with larger systems and shows the importance of standards within an installation;
- readability: the extent to which the reader is able to identify the coded functions of a program.

Readability has been the subject of a number of studies, for example De Young and Kampen (1979) have tried to develop a formula for the readability of program code, based only on countable properties of the code divided into the following five groups:

- program variables;
- comments;
- parameters of structural complexity;
- 'software science' parameters;
- program size.

Examples of such properties are:

- number of statement lines (NSL);
- mean normalised length of a variable name (VAR);
- number of operators and operands (NU1, NU2);
- frequency of operators and operands (N1, N2);
- number of comment lines (NC);
- aggregate number of program branches + 1 (CYCLO).

NSL, VAR and CYCLO proved in experiment to be the best predictors. Predictable readability (R) can be represented by the following regression equation:

$$R = +\ 0.295\ \text{VAR} - 0.499\ \text{NSL} + 0.013\ \text{CYCLO}$$

Another experiment introduced additional properties whose values could only be determined by people:

- adequate use of procedures (PRCDR);
- adequacy of comments (CMNTS);
- well-structured control flow (CNTRL).

This has confirmed the hypothesis that CNTRL is a highly significant estimation variable. Although structural complexity is also shown by CYCLO, the subjective CNTRL indicates better the influence of structural complexity.

Modifiability – Complexity, which is also discussed under 'Testability', is obviously one of the main factors affecting the modifiability of a program. Belady and Lehmann (1976, 1980) discussed this characteristic in searching for so-called 'evolution laws' allowing one to predict the effort required for modification.

Yau and Collofello (1979) have investigated the follow-up modifications which may result from a single modification in one module. Their 'Logical Stability Measure' records the ripple effects resulting from a modification. The sum of the complexity values (based on McCabe's (1976) Cyclomatic Number described below under 'Testability') for the modules affected gives the logical complexity measure for the variable. Further consideration of the probability of the variable change leads to the logical stability measure for the module. The logical stability measure for the program is the sum of the stability measures for the modules. The assumptions forming the basis for the stability measure are of doubtful validity in the absence of external validation, particularly the assumption that the probability of the modification is the same for all variables of a module and for all modules of a program. We would prefer to see some validation of the measure on real maintenance cases.

Testability – The following sub-characteristics have been considered by various writers:

- simplicity/complexity;
- modularity/structuredness;
- accessibility;
- instrumentation;

— self-descriptiveness.

What we need is an evaluation of the effort required for testing a program or some measure of the effectiveness of the test.

McCabe's Complexity Measure, otherwise known as the Cyclomatic Number, was devised for measuring the complexity of programs in order to assess their testability. The complexity (V [G]) of a program or module, ie the number of independent paths through it, is deduced from the simple equation:

$$V(G) = e - n + 2p$$

where:

e = number of edges in the control graph

n = number of vertices in the control graph

p = number of connected components

Yin (1980) has developed his *'Independence Metric',* looking at the complexity of designs to identify error-prone subprograms. A measure of independency is defined for a series of modules, on the basis that it is generally easier to carry out tests if there are many 'independent areas', that is areas consisting of an input module and all successor modules which can only be reached by call sequences passing through the input module. Testability is interrelated with:

— the number of independent areas;

— the size of these areas;

— the complexity both within and between these areas.

Without the 'Testability Analysis' system developed by Yin, manual computation would be difficult. The formula will be found in Appendix 1.

Other testability measures are presented by Mohanty and Adamowicz (1976), Paige (1980), Pimont and Rault (1976) and Woodward et al (1980).

3.3.2 Adaptability

Most software products require adaptation at some time due to changes in the operating environment. Adaptability is characterised by the effort required for such adaptation.

Programs that do not use standard interfaces to the environment or that do not use generally known details of the environment are likely to be difficult to adapt. There are strong links here with portability and re-usability. But other than general guidelines to adopt standardisation, there are no measures that specifically address this problem.

3.3.3 Expandability

Once a program is operational, particularly when it is considered to be useful by many people, requests for new functions or modifications will occur. The effort required depends not only on the type of requirement but also on the structure and clarity of the product.

Parnas (1979) advocates that a software system should be conceived during the design phase in such a way that extensions and simplification, by removing functions no longer required, can be carried out. This is often complicated by a number of facts:

- too many programs are written by people who know of design decisions not recorded in the specification;
- modules form a chain of interrelated components none of which can be removed;
- components support more than one function;
- there can be loops in the 'call' relation of certain modules.

For improvement a number of suggestions are made:

- in the early design phases it is important to form independent subsets fulfilling specific requirements;
- any unnecessary information can be hidden behind interfaces (but properly documented);
- it may be possible to solve the problem by the concept of the 'virtual machine';
- defining the way in which modules call each other in a structured manner early in the design will help to realise this concept.

Maekawa (1980) has attempted to measure extensibility in distributed computing systems as a function of the connection between the individual subsystems. His formula for system extensibility (X) is:

$$X = d(I/R)/dN$$

where R denotes the quotient of performance and cost and N the number of system components. System performance is defined by:

$$NP\ (C/(C + CrW)) = NP\ (1/(1 + rW))$$

where:

P = the performance of an individual component

C = seconds

W = the mean delay between two random components of the system

r = the frequency with which the components correspond per time unit, independently of N

CrW = the total time (execution time) of a work of C seconds in a single component

To sum up, we believe that expandability is supported by strict modularisation, exact interface definition, stability by explicit parameter transfer at the interfaces and non-total utilisation of system resources. Further practical ideas are discussed by Longworth (1983).

3.4 PRODUCT TRANSITION

The third of the types of use which we need to consider is that of product transition. It will not affect many installations whose software is designed only to run on their own computer, but even they may be affected by the use of packaged software which has been written for one computer and transferred to another. Several developments, in particular the widespread use of minicomputer and microcomputer systems, suggest that transition is now coming to be of greater importance, especially to producers of software products. Increases in networking are likely to increase this pressure. The three sub-characteristics we would like to look at are portability, re-usability and interoperability.

3.4.1 Portability

Portability is an important quality requirement in any sphere where standardised software is considered. It can be measured by the effort required to transfer a software product from one configuration to another.

The only measure available is Gilb's Portability Measure (Gilb, 1977). This requires that the resources needed to build the system on the first machine should be known and that a figure for the resources needed to transfer the system onto the target machine should also be available. The formula is:

$$PS = 1 - (ET/ER)$$

where:

PS = portability (ease of conversion from one environment to another)

ET = resources needed to move system 's' to the target environment

ER = resources needed to create system 's' for the resident environment

(The resources must be in the same units, eg costs, man-days, time, etc.)

If the measure is used as an 'after the event' indicator, it will be as objective as the details of the resources provided, but its accuracy as a predictor will depend on the accuracy of estimation of the resources needed for conversion.

McCall et al (1977) have decomposed portability in order to allow predictive evaluation on the basis of product properties as follows:

Modularity can be best obtained if:

- a hierarchical structure is available;
- no module contains more than 100 statements;
- each funtion is realised in a single module or subset of modules.

Self-descriptiveness is influenced by:

- the number and structure of comments;
- the programming language used (especially the meaningfulness of data names, module names, etc).

Machine independence is indicated by:

- use of programming languages available on other systems;
- whether the data representation is independent of the hardware configuration.

Software system independence can be realised if:

- use is made of standard operating systems, where available;
- the code does not resort to (non-standard) system utility routines;
- the modules do not contain CALL accesses to the operating system;
- common, standardised language constructs are used.

3.4.2 Re-usability

In this context emphasis is placed on individual components which may be used also as modules for the implementation of other systems. We must look therefore for product properties which facilitate the further use of individual components in other systems.

It is however difficult to find any objectively measurable quantity to characterise re-usability. One might compare, after the event, the effort required for re-using a component with the cost of producing it in the first place.

It is in its generality that re-usability differs from portability. It can be secured by not mixing input, processing and output functions in the same modules, by not mixing application and machine-dependent functions and by ensuring that where possible parameters are utilised rather than specific global variables used.

It would be interesting also to measure the efficiency of generalised modules against application specific ones.

The other sub-characteristics which might be considered are modularity, self-descriptiveness, machine independence and software/system independence.

3.4.3 Interoperability

In the original GE model this characteristic was particularly related to the interaction of programs in computer networks. In any installation, however, there can be problems in getting data commonality and communication between systems sorted out.

The following properties are among those which will have a strong bearing on whether systems can operate successfully together:

- modular structure of programs;
- standardised rules of program coupling (interface specification);
- standardised data representation pattern;
- good standards of documentation and inter-system communication.

It is not a characteristic for which specific measures have been proposed, though modularity measures such as Gilb's 'Structural Complexity Measure' (Gilb, 1977) and Myers' 'Module Independence Measure' (Myers, 1976) could be considered.

4 Multidimensional Software Quality Evaluation

4.1 THE NATURE OF MULTIDIMENSIONAL EVALUATION

After obtaining measurements or making realistic predictions of measurements, we soon realise that this is not enough. All that we are able to do with the measurements is to compare them with results from previous programs or with estimates. Nearly always we are restricted to consideration only of the single property or sub-characteristic; only very rarely does this permit us to look at a single undivided characteristic. We are still a long way from finding the overall quality. Also when we have the objective measurements, we still have to know what values are 'good' with respect to the particular purpose we have in mind.

So we have to perform two steps. Firstly, we must map the raw scores onto a judgement scale in order to derive a required utility score, below which the program or product must be regarded as less than suitable with respect to this particular property. Secondly, we have to combine the individual judgements as described in this chapter. This will itself normally be a two-stage procedure as it is necessary to combine the sub-characteristics into a judgement for the whole characteristic and then to combine all these judgements into a single judgement of the quality of the whole program.

If there are no objective measures available, one has to make an evaluation direct onto the judgement scales for the product properties or sub-characteristics. Again, if the judgements are carried out by several people, extra steps will be needed to combine the individual judgements.

For all these amalgamations, there are a number of multidimensional methods available, some of which will be described in this chapter.

They are used at a number of points in the development life cycle:

- Before the start it is necessary to define what measurement and evaluation procedures will be adopted and what levels of these measures will be considered sufficient. Thus, a target level for the evaluation can be set.
- At each stage of the life cycle a predictive evaluation may be carried out for relevant sub-characteristics and at the completion of the stage a compliance evaluation should be carried out.
- At the end, both during acceptance tests and after a period of live running, a full evaluation of the overall quality of the product or system should be carried out.

4.2 SOME MULTIDIMENSIONAL METHODS

The following methods will be discussed:

- polarity profile;
- simple scoring;
- weighted scoring;
- phased weighting;
- Kepner-Tregoe Method;
- Cologne Combination Method

4.2.1 Polarity Profile

The polarity profile is based on the *semantic differential,* which is widely used in social sciences as a measure of attitude. It appears to be well suited for measuring multidimensional constructs.

The measurement process involves rating the concept on a series of polar attributes, which form a graduated scale from −3 on one side through zero (as the neutral point) to +3 on the other. Each category can be labelled by adverb qualifiers, for example:

extremely complex	−3
complex	−2
slightly complex	−1

neither complex nor simple	0
slightly simple	+1
simple	+2
extremely simple	+3

It is often assumed that the intervals within the scales are equal, as this facilitates further amalgamation (as described below). The negative scores are given to the unwanted attributes.

In order to measure an object/concept, the measurer marks the position on each scale which indicates the direction and intensity of his opinion.

To use the polarity profile method for evaluating the quality of software, each quality characteristic is broken down into sub-characteristics, and polar adjective pairs are formed for each. After the rating procedure has been carried out the sum of the scores is averaged to find the position on the scale for the whole characteristic. This would assume that each sub-characteristic was of equal value.

The polarity profile for reliability could look like this:

+	+3	+2	+1	0	−1	−2	−3	−
accurate	X							inaccurate
tolerant (of errors)		X						intolerant
consistent	X							inconsistent
simple				X				complex

Averaging the reliability scores (in this case the average is 2) for transfer to the higher level profile conceals the variability of their individual profiles. This could become a problem when comparing the overall profile with the quality requirements.

So our final example is again simplified, since in practice we might want to consider the underlying profile shape as well. What we have is a compliance evaluation looking at the five quality characteristics considered in Section 3.2 for the product operation:

+	+3	+2	+1	0	−1	−2	−3	−
usable		X	*					unusable
secure	X				*			insecure
efficient	*	X						inefficient
correct		X	*					incorrect
reliable		X*						unreliable

The X-X-X line represents the required quality. The *-*-* line represents the actual quality, formed either by amalgamation of lower-level profiles (or possibly by using the subjective rating of the characteristic as a whole). In this case, security (integrity) needs most improvement, usability and correctness need some improvement, and too much efficiency has been achieved, probably at the expense of the other characteristics. Thus, overall, the required quality has not been reached.

A polarity profile provides reliable information only if it can be compared with at least one of the following:

- judgements of the same program at another time;
- judgements of a comparative object (eg two packages to do the same task);
- an 'ideal' program, ie with the required quality (as in our example). It would be possible also to specify the requirements in terms of the *ideal* and the *minimum* required quality on the same profile. The actual quality would then have to lie between the two.

In each of these comparisons, high similarity between profiles indicates:

- stability over a period of time (it might indicate 'no improvement'; stability is not necessarily 'good');
- high similarity of quality between two programs;
- good compliance of actual quality with required quality.

To sum up, the polarity profile evaluation method is quite clear and economical, especially where all sub-characteristics are seen to be of equal importance. It can be helpful to have the diagrammatic representation.

4.2.2 Utility Analyses

Simple Scoring

This is the simplest available method of evaluation. All that is required is a score on a judgement scale for each characteristic to be considered. On the recommended scale, 1 is the lowest level and 7 the highest. These scores are then added together to give a combined utility score for the overall quality.

For compliance evaluation, there will also be a target utility score to compare with the achieved utility score, while for comparative evaluation there will be two products (programs) to compare against each other (and perhaps against an 'ideal' or a minimum level). This method assumes all characteristics are of equal weight and it ignores (or hides) any cases where one characteristic is higher than another since one good score balances a bad one on a quite different characteristic. Only the user can decide whether this is satisfactory in a particular case. The methods which follow take account of these points.

A deliberate over-simplification concerns how to convert measures or values for properties or sub-characteristics on to the judgement scale for the characteristic as a whole. We do not recommend the use of any specific technique. It may be possible to convert the measure for each attribute to a judgement scale which can then be used to provide an average for the characteristic of which the attributes are part. For some attributes this is easy, where, for example, there is either a measurement scale which is itself graduated in such a way that the transformation is obvious or where it is known what values on (say) a 'complexity' scale are to be considered 'high' or 'low'. It may, however, be necessary for the user to take a view of such a measure based on his experience, or to take a view on the characteristic as a whole based on the average of other properties. (This could be difficult if there happen to be a number of such measures against one characteristic.)

Simple scoring can be further varied by specifying target scores for the individual criteria.

4.2.3 Weighted Scoring

This method (which has also been called the 'multifactor' method) can utilise weighted criteria.

Having amalgamated the properties to the judgement scale for the characteristics, the score achieved is multiplied by the weighting factor (which should be taken form a restricted interval, eg the same 1-7 scale as used for scoring). There is of course no objection to two characteristics being given the same weight if they are considered to be of equal importance. The scores are then combined to give an overall evaluation score by adding the scores as converted by the weights. The method of comparing with target scores or with other programs is the same as for 'simple scoring'.

4.2.4 Phased Weighting Factor Method

As implied in its name, the 'phased weighting factor' method is an extension of the previous method. It is based on a phasing by combining individual criteria to criteria groups. There is therefore an additional level of weighting.

Having achieved a weighted score, as in the previous method, the characteristics are divided into groups (three groups will usually be sufficient) each of which is given its own weight. The group weight is multiplied by the sum of the weighted scores within the group, to produce a group score which is added to the other group scores to give a total utility score which is then compared with the required utility score or with other programs or products. The effect of this two-stage weighting is to increase the influence of characteristics in the highest rated groups pro-rata to the group weights. It is not clear at what point sufficient data is available to allow users to decide rationally how to divide their ratings in this way. Sub-characteristics could be weighted and combined into groups corresponding to the single characteristics (one might need more than three groups in this case).

It is suggested for convenience that the weights within each group and of each group might be percentages.

4.2.5 The Kepner-Tregoe Method

The Kepner-Tregoe Method (Kepner and Tregoe, 1981) is a method of decision analysis which has been used for software quality evaluation, being suitable for solving multidimensional evaluation problems. It is to some extent similar to the weighting factor method, with one specific characteristic in addition.

The first step of this method consists of sorting the criteria according to their degree of importance. It is necessary to differentiate between essential criteria (or necessary requirements) and desirable criteria. These may be either at the level of characteristics or of product properties. It is necessary that specific minimum values on the measurement scales should be specified for the essential criteria. Any product which does not achieve the specified value for all the essential criteria is considered unsuitable for the purpose under consideration, so that it is not necessary to measure or evaluate the other characteristics.

The desirable requirements are converted to a utility score by the use of the weighting factor method. Kepner and Tregoe suggest the use of a scale from 1 to 10 for these weights, though there is no particular reason why this should be any better than the 1 to 7 scale we have recommended earlier.

The method suggests that this should be only a provisional decision and recommends continued assessment of the actual use in order to provide more detailed quality criteria that could be used in a new evaluation process. This may allow negative secondary effects to be minimised.

4.2.6 The Cologne Combination Method

Unlike the other methods which have been described the Cologne Combination Method (Schmitz et al, 1975) has been developed on the basis of a successive series of comparisons of quality characteristics. It is thus more suitable for comparison of a group of alternatives than for compliance evaluation of one product with a standard or ideal.

We do however start with a similar list of quality characteristics, which are to be divided into suitable areas according to 'content-oriented dependencies. Thus we might, for example, divide the quality characteristics into the three areas already considered, of operation, revision and transition, or into reliability, maintainability and testability which are related to simplicity/complexity. Our example chooses the former option.

Having thus divided characteristics into areas, of which there should be as few as possible, it is necessary to classify each characteristic according to its order of importance. This in known, for reasons which will become clear, as the 'abandonment rank order'. The least important is given the value 1, the next 2 and so on. Subsequently the procedure is applied to the characteristics within each area and then to the areas themselves (Table 4.1).

Product area	Characteristic	Abandonment rank order
	Usability Correctness Reliability Security Efficiency	5 4 3 2 1
Operation		3
	Maintainability Adaptability Expandability	3 2 1
Revision		2
	Portability Re-usability Interoperability	3 2 1
Transition		1

Table 4.1 Abandonment Rank Order

The next step is to consider each characteristic in turn. It is necessary to compare each product with the next in order to decide which is of the higher quality. This may be done by a similar evaluation procedure to that discussed previously; the difference, and possibly advantage, of this method is that it is necessary only to rank the characteristics without quantifying the differences, which should involve less work. It is of course possible to use a further stage of the Cologne Combination Method for the evaluation of the sub-characteristics and their amalgamation into a rank order for the characteristic as a whole. We will end up with a matrix as in Table 4.2.

The results of paired comparison are shown in Table 4.3.

Product area	Characteristic	Rank order of alternatives A	B	C
Operation	Usability	3	1	2
	Correctness	1	2	3
	Reliability	2	1	2
	Security	1	1	1
	Efficiency	3	1	2
Revision	Maintainability	3	2	1
	Adaptability	1	3	2
	Expandability	2	1	3
Transition	Portability	1	3	2
	Re-usability	3	2	1
	Interoperability	2	1	3

Table 4.2 Rank Order of Alternatives

Product area	Characteristic	Paired comparison A-B	A-C	B-C
	Usability	A	A	C
	Correctness	B	C	C
	Reliability	A	—	C
	Security	—	—	—
	Efficiency	A	A	C
Operation		A	A	C
	Maintainability	A	A	B
	Adaptability	B	C	B
	Expendability	A	C	C
Revision		A	C	B
	Portability	B	C	B
	Re-usability	A	A	B
	Interoperability	A	C	C
Transition		A	C	B

A — indicates equal ranking

Table 4.3 Paired Comparisons

Within each of the criteria areas, the number of superordinations should be counted using the so-called 'majority rule'. The abandonment rank order is used (a) in cases of doubt and (b) for verifying the result of the majority rule test. In our example, in the area of 'product operation', using both the majority rule test and the abandonment rank order, the product A is plainly superior. In the other two areas the situation is different, since each product is superior to one of the others by two superordinations to one. The way to resolve this is by use of the abandonment rank order. Thus for 'product revision', Product A is seen to be superior because it is superior to both the other products at the highest level; for 'product transition' it is Product B which is superior. It is now seen that by a further comparison of the areas themselves, Product A has the highest number of superordinations and is the preferred choice in the 'product operation' group, which is the highest of the three groups. Finally it is reasonable to check the individual results and the whole procedure again, particularly for consistency and significance.

There may of course be other grounds for choice not included in the above. It does not, for example, take into account 'cost'. This can either be seen as a factor to be used when shortlisting candidate products or it could be included as a separate criterion to be allocated a suitable lot in one of the three areas. The result will depend where it is allocated which confirms that the method allows us to put as much weight as we like on any individual factor.

5 Evaluation of Software Production Aids

5.1 QUALITY CHARACTERISTICS OF SOFTWARE PRODUCTION AIDS

In considering the meaning and measurement of 'quality' in the context of a methodology (eg for defining systems requirements or for systems design), it is possible to discover a set of quality characteristics which together describe its quality as seen by the user. This 'external' view of the methodology comprises a common set of all the aspects or things which are important for all the usages, whether by business analysts, systems analysts, user representatives, designers, quality engineers or managers.

We will show later in this chapter how these characteristics can be used in the practical evaluation of the quality of the aids to the development of software products. Pioneering work in this area has been done by G Rzevski (Law, 1983). The quality attributes which he proposes are:

- relevance;
- reliability;
- efficiency;
- maintainability;
- usability;
- robustness;
- social acceptability;
- elegance.

It will at once be seen that this set shares characteristics with those already discussed as applicable to software products. This is not surprising since the quality of the methodology depends very largely on the quality of the software ultimately produced. For neatness, it might have seemed preferable to force the characteristics into the same framework as described previously (relevance, social acceptability and elegance might perhaps be contained in usability). Since however the work which has been done uses the set given above, it is worth considering briefly the meaning of each.

Relevance

'Relevance' is both complex and important; methodology is not worth further consideration unless it is relevant. It may be informally defined as 'the extent to which the methodology meets the real needs of those defining requirements or designing systems.'

Relevance may be assessed by relating the features of each methodology under consideration to:

- the attributes and features of the work products resulting from the development activity;
- the attributes and features of the process of defining requirements or designing systems which are relevant to the particular development organisation.

Thus the developer needs to consider the structurability, applicability, correctness, completeness, reliability, efficiency, usability and robustness of the product and the correctness, completeness, power and efficiency of the process of developing systems for his or her organisation.

Reliability

The reliability of a methodology may be regarded as the probability that it will achieve its claims consistently over many uses, or that there will be a low occurrence of errors during those uses. It may be assessed by looking for evidence that the claims made for a methodology are well founded; for example the techniques and tools used should be known to be effective and used correctly within their proper domains of application and within a coherent overall structure.

Reliability may be considered in the following areas:

- experience in use;
- structure, including validity of both general and problem-oriented constructs and their use;
- control over development activities.

Efficiency

There are several issues involved in the efficiency of a methodology. If a methodology is effective in achieving quality in its products, this may well result in a reduction of the total effort required to achieve any given level of quality. Equally, the methodology may actually require more effort at the early stages than a competitor, even though the total effort required will be less; for example, to anyone considering only the requirements specification in isolation, the methodology may appear less efficient. The resolution of these issues lies in regarding efficiency as the 'total amount of resource used per 'unit' of product of the desired quality'. The figure for total resources must include those which will be needed in later stages because of deficiencies in the specification.

Maintainability

'Maintainability' may be regarded as the inverse of the effort required to keep the methodology itself up to date and to modify it to suit changing needs. Factors influencing maintainability include:

- understandability;
- structuredness;
- open-endedness;
- level of support;
- degrees of computerisation;
- change control procedures.

Usability

'Usability' is also an inverse measure, of the effort and knowledge required in order to learn and use the methodology. It will be affected by the following aspects of the methodology:

- understandability;

- accessibility;
- level of training support;
- the standard of man-machine interfaces.

Robustness

Robustness can be regarded as a measure of the resistance of the methodology to misuse (it is thus not the same as reliability). One would expect to find such features as:

- clear sequencing of tasks;
- specified checkpoints;
- 'restrictive' tools and procedures (which restrain the user from certain courses of action).

Social Acceptability

'Social acceptability' can be regarded as the degree to which the methodology will be welcomed by analysts and others involved in defining requirements or designing systems. If a methodology is not acceptable to its users, there is unlikely to be the commitment to its use necessary to achieve success. It is therefore advisable that there should be procedures for 'selling' and introducing the methodology.

Elegance

'Elegance' is perhaps too subjective a quality to measure. And yet a methodology may be more effective in providing solutions for complex problems if it is itself ingeniously simple. Such an elegant methodology will also help to generate a powerful sense of comprehension in its users.

5.2 A RECURSIVE APPROACH TO THE QUALITY EVALUATION OF METHODOLOGIES FOR SYSTEMS DESIGN

5.2.1 Background

There is an urgent need for 'methods for comparing methods' (André et al, 1980, pp 6 and 68). Software development organisations are concerned with the evaluation and selection of those methodologies which will be cost effective over a timescale of five to ten years. The methodologies are often very complex and difficult to understand (especially before they have been tried) and are hence also difficult to compare.

The ideal method of comparing alternative software development methodologies would be to produce the same software object to the same level of quality using each alternative method, and to compare the resources consumed over the lifetime of the object. Obviously, this procedure would be uneconomical in terms of time and cost. In practice it is necessary to resort to paper assessment, trials on small and probably unrepresentative problems and the reported experiences of others in comparable situations. Not only are such reports not easy to obtain, but it is also difficult to be certain that the situations are truly comparable. The more candidate aids there are, the more need there is for a quick and economical method of selection.

5.2.2 A Multi-level Selection Procedure

A multi-level approach to selection seems appropriate, like those used in marketing for the assessment of suggestions for new or improved products.

The first level is the 'coarse screen' elimination of unsuitable candidates. The attributes of each candidate are compared against a list of desired attributes. The aim is to elicit the 'observables' which when combined form the quality characteristic 'relevance'. It is important that information about each candidate can be quickly and easily obtained from a salesman or supporting documentation. (The mechanics of this process are discussed in Section 5.3).

The second level of assessment is the 'fine screen' elimination of candidates by closer examination. This is achieved by expressing these critical characteristics in terms of their 'observable components' and searching for evidence that the candidates either possess or in some way support these components.

Having reduced the number of apparently suitable candidates as far as possible (and if there is still more than one candidate left), the final stage of evaluation is to compare them in terms which should provide a good prediction of their relative performance in the intended application. Possible techniques at this stage are performance of test problems, ranking of characteristics and assessing reported performance from reference applications.

This multi-level selection procedure poses two major questions:

- can the quality characteristics be defined clearly and completely in terms of a reasonable set of 'observable properties'?
- can these characteristics be quickly and easily evaluated?

We are looking for evaluation techniques which are based on relevant properties which are verifiable. Such techniques should:

- be based on simple, visible tests;
- be based on available test results;
- be based on available documentation;
- be objective;
- give repeatable results;
- be valid, in the sense of being good predictors of good performance;
- require minimum use of expert knowledge.

5.2.3 Some Attribute-based Approaches

A number of evaluation 'frameworks' have been proposed based on different but overlapping sets of attributes of development methodologies and the environment in which they are to be used. A coherent methodology is regarded as 'a system of technical methods and management procedures that covers the entire development activity' (Freeman and Wasserman, 1982). The management and technical elements in a methodology should reinforce one another.

In the UK Department of Industry (1981) study into software development methodologies for use with the Ada language, 13 groups of attributes were identified and classified into five major categories (Table 5.1).

In the US Department of Defence (DOD) sponsored study on the same subject (Freeman and Wasserman, 1982), 12 high-level requirements for a methodology were identified:

- cover the entire development process;
- enhance communication among interested parties;
- support problem analysis and understanding;

- support for 'top-down' and 'bottom-up' development;
- support for validation and verification;
- support for constraints;
- support for the software development organisation (ie project aspects);
- support for system evolution;
- automated support (ie computer-based tools);
- software configuration management;
- teachability and transferability;
- open-endedness.

The DOD study further identified four main categories of attributes that a methodology should possess to support its claims to meet these requirements:

- technical attributes, ie features that pertain to support of various desirable technical concepts such as function hierarchy, data hierarchy, data abstraction, etc;

Category	Attribute group
Development life cycle	Relations to the major development phases of the methodology's own life cycle model
Technical aspects	Notations Procedures Automated tools Checking
Project aspects	Configuration control Management
Use of the methodology	Experience Applicability Transferability
Compatibility with Ada	Specific characteristics pertinent to Ada language

Table 5.1 Software Attributes

- usage attributes, ie features relating to the methodology application to development situations;
- management attributes, ie factors relating to the ability to improve the management of software development;
- economic attributes, eg monetary benefits and costs of acquisition, use and management.

Looking at methodologies for producing an intermediate product, in this case a requirements specification, the UK National Economic Development Office Working Group (NEDO81) took a task-oriented approach. Relevant attributes of a methodology are those which indicate its usefulness in supporting each task. The tasks involved in specifying requirements were categorised by viewpoints:

User view:

- define informal and precise statement;
- detailed functions of systems and detail of its environment;
- functional structure of system and data;
- define product quality attributes.

Design view:

- unambiguous definition of system to be designed and implemented;
- establish feasibility of requirements specification;
- analyse and decompose system function.

Quality view:

- analyse formal statement for consistency and completeness;
- define formal tasks to check implementation against specification.

Control view:

- management through the development stages of large amounts of information defining the product.

Supplementing the task-oriented attributes, a number of general attributes were identified:

- compatibility with the method of later development phases;
- ease of learning, introduction and use;
- maturity and stability;
- availability of local support;
- cost of acquisition;

The Kingston Polytechnic approach is another instance of a framework approach, but differs from the examples given above in that it has a single, coherent viewpoint, namely 'quality', for finding attributes. The quality of a software design methodology is viewed in relation to the needs of a design organisation as pursuing two aims:

- to improve the productivity of designers;
- to help achieve the desired quality of the design products.

5.3 THE METHOD

5.3.1 Introduction

We now explore in more detail what has to be done, what is the justification for some of the procedures and also attempt to explain why it is called a 'recursive approach'.

It must be noted that the approach is concerned with criteria for the selection of the most cost-effective methodologies for particular design organisations. Therefore it considers first what is required by a design organisation and then how to select a methodology which best meets those requirements.

Any evaluation must be based on judging the capabilities of methodologies to meet these aims and comparing their costs. Since few organisations would be prepared to apply competing methodologies to a set of carefully selected design problems, we have devised a more economical, though less precise, way of comparing design methodologies, based on the assessment of the quality characteristics of each. The work of devising the approach and the questionnaire used was done by G Rzevski (Law, 1983).

5.3.2 The Questionnaire Approach

The method chosen uses a questionnaire; the questions used in the first trial of this approach are applicable to system design methodologies. For other types of software development aide adaptation is necessary, and some work on this has been done within the context of requirements definition methods (Law, 1984).

Relevance

The method is as follows:

- the user answers the questions which cover his requirements;
- a number of methodologies are assessed for 'scope' by means of a matching set of questions;
- the answers are transferred to the 'relevance graph' (Figure 5.1), which is used to provide a visual match. Those methodologies which appear to match best are chosen to form a short list. In selecting the short list the following points should be taken into consideration:

  • not all the features on the relevance forms merit equal rating in all circumstances, so a simple comparison of areas on the relevance graph may not be appropriate;

  • the scope of the methodology is that claimed by the vendors, unless there is available an independent view, and is not yet necessarily verified.

At this stage, the user has considered only relevance, by considering some features of the design products which will be produced and some features of the design process involved.

Features of design products

For the purpose of selecting the best methodology for the design of a particular class of product, such as information systems or compilers, it is convenient to group product features under the following five headings:

- size;
- application orientation;
- architecture;
- components;

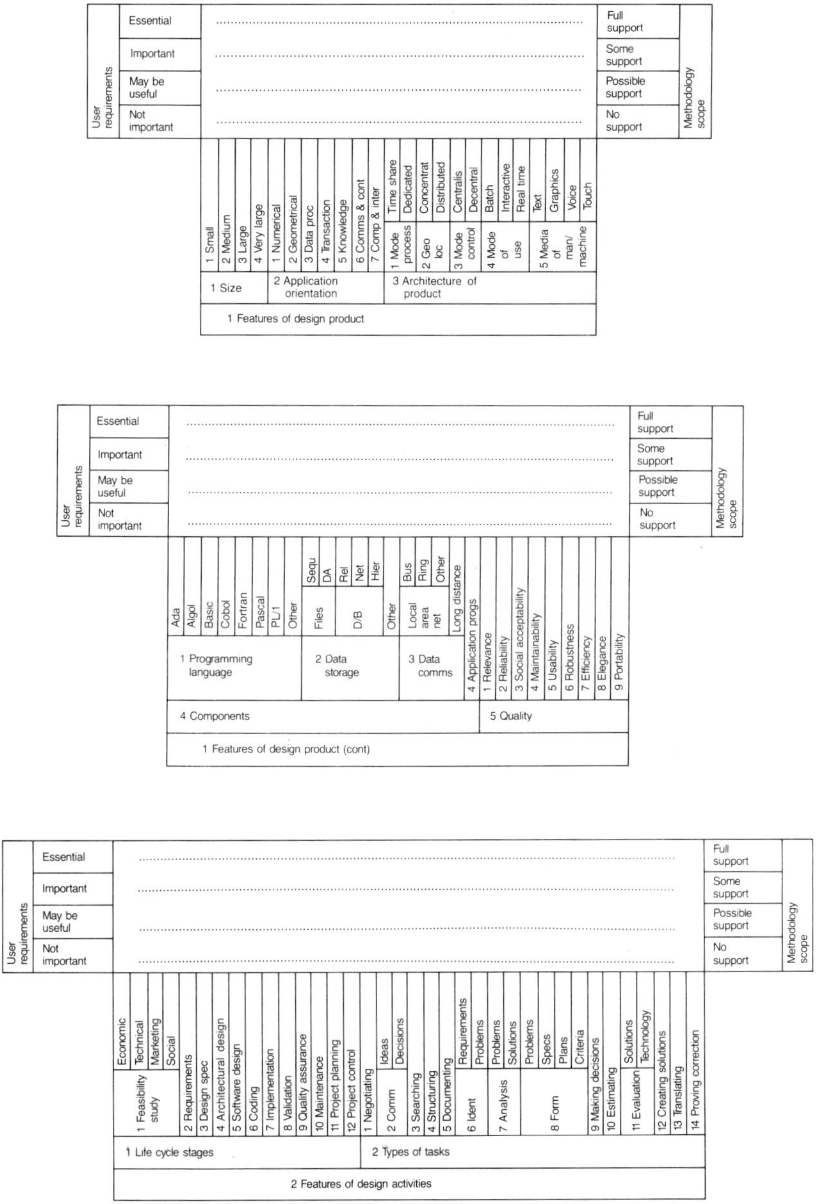

Figure 5.1 Relevance Graph

- quality.

Size: although any decision based on size is arbitrary, since the point at which software goes in one class rather than another is often unclear, there is no doubt that software of different sizes may require different design methods. For example, small programs, requiring approximately three person-months of effort, will require from a methodology little more than help with data structuring and functional decomposition; whereas larger programs may need project planning and control support, requirements analysis support, specification and design support, data network and database design, computer-based tools such as data dictionaries and software engineering databases, etc.

Application orientation: products for different types of applications are as a rule characterised by different features and may therefore require different design methods and tools.

Product architecture: the 'architecture' is here defined as the collection of all those aspects of a system that directly affect the organisation within which it operates, eg:

- mode of processing;
- geographical location;
- mode of control;
- mode of use;
- medium of man-machine communication.

Product components: it is convenient to describe the needs of designers and features of methodologies in terms of the following components:

- languages;
- data storage components (type of files/databases);
- data communication components (eg local networks, long distance communications).

Product quality: it would be possible to consider product quality (as Rzevski, 1980, does) in terms of the same quality characteristics as he uses for the quality of methodologies. We would prefer to see this consideration in terms of those characteristics which we have defined for software product quality.

Features of the design process

It is necessary to consider both design activities and design tasks.

Design activities: even though strictly speaking we are concerned only with the design process, it is useful to assess the relevance of methodologies in respect of all software lifecycle activities. The activities considered will depend on the lifecycle model in current use, so the following are examples only:

- feasibility study;
- requirements analysis;
- requirements specification;
- global design;
- detailed design;
- coding;
- implementation;
- validation (testing);
- acceptance;
- maintenance;
- project planning;
- project control.

Design tasks: examples of types of tasks, which may occur in any lifecycle activity are:

- negotiating;
- communicating (ideas, decisions);
- searching (for information);
- structuring (information);
- documenting (decisions);
- identifying (requirements, problems);
- analysing (problems, proposed solutions);
- formulating (plans, criteria, specifications);

- making decisions;
- estimating;
- measuring;
- evaluating;
- creating tentative solutions;
- translating from informal into formal languages;
- proving correctness;
- transforming one model into another.

Different design organisations are likely to view the activities of design differently and to require methodological support for different types of design task. It is therefore necessary to find out which ones any specific methodology supports. This will of course not be of such importance where the design organisation does not have its own view — it might be prepared to accept a methodology which suits it in other ways, without considering design tasks at all.

The method now goes on to consider the short list of methodologies which pass the first screening process. Having assured themselves that the methodologies are relevant, the users go on to consider the other quality characteristics defined in Figure 5.1, namely:

- reliability;
- efficiency;
- maintainability;
- usability;
- robustness;
- social acceptability;
- elegance.

Reliability

In considering the reliability of a methodology, one needs to consider:

- the underlying principles and assumptions;

- the consitituent concepts, methods, procedures and guidelines, including their relations to the underlying principles;
- the supporting tools offered, including the constraints that they impose upon the design process;
- past success in practical applications.

The questionnaire attempts to discover what is present in a given methodology.

A methodology is likely to be reliable only if it is based on sound principles, such as:

- separation of concern;
- stepwise refinement;
- perceivability;
- completeness and lack of ambiguity;
- user-centred design;
- implementation-independent design;
- evolution;
- minimising interconnectedness;
- reinforcement by providing immediate feedback.

The method will discover what concepts, methods, procedures and guidelines have been derived from the principles in order to give people direct help in solving design problems. These may be technical or management concepts, listed below:

Technical concepts;

- explicit definition and modelling of the environment in which software will be placed;
- definition of information required, including logical structure, time and location, and of the processes which have to be performed on data;
- stepwise refinement of both data and processes in order that the final work product is perceivable;
- clear distinction between systems analysis (definition and

modelling of environment) and design;

- design of data structures and algorithms in such a way that they are reasonably independent.

Management concepts:

- stepwise refinement into perceivable tasks, with explicit definition of work products;
- validation of work products immediately after their completion;
- independent validation;
- emphasis on fault avoidance methods;
- consultation and preferably direct involvement of the prospective users of the methodology.

It is also important, for the reliability of a methodology, that it should possess a comprehensive set of manual and computer tools. These will not only help to increase the productivity of designers but will also prevent designers making mistakes and pursuing incorrect design procedures. Such tools include:

- well-designed forms;
- structured diagram languages;
- data dictionaries;
- interactive software design tools;
- documentation generators.

Efficiency

In looking for efficiency, given our definition of the quality of a methodology, we want to improve the productivity of design. Major improvements in productivity can only be achieved by concentrating resources on the analysis, specification and design stages with a view to saving time and cost later. The key methods for productivity improvements are *fault avoidance* and *fault removal* methods; broadly speaking, they will also contribute to high reliability and maintainability.

For this reason, our questionnaire examines how well the methodologies support fault avoidance and removal. Specifically we look for the ways in which each methodology:

- keeps the design task and software work product under control;
- ensures that design tasks are unambiguously defined;
- ensures that documentation is complete and unambiguous;
- provides effective computer-aided design tools;
- includes adequate training procedures.

We also look for procedures for:

- inspection of work products;
- simulation of work products;
- automatic checking of computer-readable work products;
- testing and debugging of code;
- initiating, performing, and documenting modifications.

At this point in the evaluation process we look at certain constituents of the methodology which may have an effect on particular characteristics of the final software product. We give examples of some of these, listing them in the questionnaire under product relevance, product efficiency, product usability, etc.

Maintainability

We look at such factors as:

- the complexity of a methodology and its documentation;
- the level of support available;
- the degree of computerisation;
- the complexity of all associated software;
- any restriction on modifications imposed.

Other characteristics

We also examine the usability, robustness, social acceptability and elegance of the methodologies under review. The final choice will depend on the relevance factors and the other quality characteristics which have already been discussed. One of the multidimensional measuring methods discussed elsewhere will need to be used to discover which software development aid has the highest quality, bearing in mind that the ranking methods can adjust for the factors considered important.

The consideration of cost must also not be forgotten, including purchase, maintenance (and other recurring costs), 'training', 'manuals', 'documentation' and 'introductory' costs.

Finally, we should mention why this has been named a recursive approach:

- it considers the software development aid at an increasing level of detail on successive passes;
- it considers the quality characteristics of the software development aid in terms of the quality characteristics of the software which is to be produced.

It is found that this induces an increasing level of confidence in the methodology which is finally chosen.

5.4 TESTING THE RECURSIVE APPROACH

The method was tested by its originators using the STRADIS methodology as a test object (Law, 1983).

An attempted independent validation, which is described more fully elsewhere (Watts, 1983), is summarised below.

It is necessary to establish the following points:

- could people use the questionnaire?
- were users able to state their requirements?
- could vendors state what their methods offered (or could existing users describe the methods they used in this form)?
- could users evaluate methods of which they had some experience?

The points should be considered in terms of the criteria of goodness discussed in Section 6.1, ie do the results show that the approach is:

- objective;
- reliable;
- valid;
- standardised;
- comparable;
- economical;
- useful.

The originators were unable to find sufficient subjects for the study with precisely the requirement of choosing a design methodology. For this reason, it was found necessary to question existing users of design methodologies. It was hoped to discover their requirements for a design methodology in the light of their experience as well as the answers to the four questions given above. It was not possible to learn, however, whether the user requirements questions were meaningful to less experienced respondents.

The form was redesigned in view of the above: user requirements, details of the methods and user rating of those methods were each given a separate column on the same form. This would not work for the 'real world' situation but was perfectly satisfactory for this purpose. It is likely that there was some halo effect — a user who rated a point highly would also say that the methodology could do this. This did not seem too important (the methodology scope and rating sections of the original questionnaire had already been completed for one methodology).

The trial shows that the approach is undoubtedly promising: it gave reasonable marks to a recognised methodology, and a structured design method was clearly better than unstructured methods, We did not, however, obtain sufficient answers to give statistically sound results, which would allow us to recommend any particular method. Nor, therefore, could we be sure that the sort of method that comes out best is really best!

The approach appears to be weakest in picking up people's requirements, so it would appear that more instruction or rewording of the questions in this area may be required. The method is still under development and later results may be more encouraging.

The reason that we recommend further employment of this approach is that we are sure that it is in advance of the usual methods of choosing software development methodologies. We believe that since it follows the consideration of the quality characteristics as recommended elsewhere in this book, it will make a reasonable choice more likely. We would like, therefore, to see more trials of this method in real-life situations.

5.5 THE FUTURE

We would like to see these comparisons and selection methods further developed. This has already been done in the context of Requirements Definition Methods (Law, 1984).

The methods could also be improved by taking into account the experience of serious users. We believe that a 'candidate' set of requirements could be set out for a number of typical organisations; we would then recommend the use of these as a starting point.

It would undoubtedly be possible to collect data in this form about all the major methodologies which could be validated against the experience of existing users of these methodologies. This would allow one to use the scope and rating forms as set down, rather than having to carry out the analysis each time. It would of course be necessary to keep this information up to date in the light of any changes to the methodologies.

This information could also be transformed into a computerised database, initially merely to display the data on demand, but eventually to carry out more sophisticated matching routines, perhaps by means of an expert system.

6 How Good Should Quality Measures Be?

Measures which are available have been discussed already in Chapter 3 and are summarised also in Appendix 1. In this chapter, we will examine both what we mean by saying that a measure is 'good', that is the criteria of 'goodness', and the procedures for validating quality measures.

6.1 CRITERIA OF 'GOODNESS' FOR SOFTWARE MEASURES

We will consider here what we mean by saying that a measure is 'good'. Following psychological testing methods, we consider that a measure is good that is methodologically suitable for supporting evaluation and decision processes, only if it is:

- objective;
- reliable;
- valid;
- standardised;
- comparable;
- economical;
- useful.

Objectivity

A measure can only be considered objective if it is free from any subjective influences of the testers.

Objectivity in *execution* indicates the extent to which the results of measuring are independent of the tester's behavior during the measuring process. Important prerequisites for achieving maximum objectivity are:

- detailed instructions for the use of the measure;
- standardised approaches to the collection of measured values.

Objectivity in *evaluation* indicates whether there is agreement among various testers in mapping measuring results onto scales.

Objectivity in *interpretation* shows the extent of agreement between testers in their analysis of the measuring results on the basis of the mapping to the scale. It has to be admitted that this part of the operation of a measure is much more difficult to control. It is obviously much better if all users of a measure agree what 'scores' are related to 'degrees of excellence', but in the last analysis it is up to the interpreter, since there may be perfectly valid reason why one installation, or even one system, should accept different scores. We have already defined quality as 'suitability for the purpose', not as the 'degree of objective excellence'.

To determine the degree of objectivity one may take a sample and calculate the mean correlation coefficient.

Reliability

Reliability indicates the degree of accuracy with which a characteristic (or an attribute or a product property) or a combination of characteristics can be measured. It is therefore a measure of the reproducibility of the measuring results; it depends on stability and precision of measuring, as well as on constancy of measuring conditions.

Reliability decreases with increasing error variance. The degree of reliability is indicated by a reliability coefficient which must not only express measuring and recording errors, but also be sensitive enough to take into account modifications of characteristics over time. Random errors occurring within the data to be measured will also have to be taken into account.

Four different methods are generally used for reliability testing:

Re-test: the same measure is applied to the same or similar samples of tested objects after an appropriate interval; correlation of a series of results may be applied.

Parallel test: two measures, which are believed to be both objective and valid, may be applied to the same sample. One reason for using this method may be that there is an existing measure which is reliable (but deficient on some other grounds) and some new measure is to be compared with it. Another situation in which it would be useful would be where the existing measure is either thought, or even known, to be unreliable and an improvement is being sought.

Split half method: where a measure can be divided into two equivalent halves, both parts may be applied to the same sample. The separate series of results can then be correlated and the 'split half consistency coefficient' determined.

Consistency analysis: if the elements of certain measures are treated as repeatedly halved measure parts, reliability is indirectly determined by statistical methods (such as analysis of variance) and expressed by a consistency coefficient. These methods can be found in standard statistics textbooks.

Validity

The validity of a measure means the extent to which a measure really measures that characteristic (or attribute) which it claims or is supposed to measure. A measure is only valid if it is justified that one should infer the real characteristics from the indicators (the observable properties). We will be looking further into validation in the next section (6.2) so that what appears here will serve as an introduction.

Various aspects of validity may be distinguished:

Content validity: the content is valid if the measure is constituted in such a way that it represents the characteristic investigated. Procedures for determining this are described in Section 6.2; these rely on the opinions of experts.

Empirical validity: this type of validity is probably the most important. The measure is compared with an 'external criterion' (external validity), with other measures already proved valid (internal validity), with expert estimates (concurrent validity), or with estimated values (predictive validity). If there is reasonable similarity between the measure and the comparison criterion, it is likely that the measure is valid. The greater the similarity, the greater is the empirical validity.

Construct validity: it is necessary to ascertain the construct validity for descriptive characteristics which cannot be determined by experimentation. This is done by proving theoretically what the measure to be considered really measures. This is best done by use of correlation and factor analysis methods, as described below (6.2).

Validity is perhaps the most important requirement for a measure. It is also the most difficult to fulfil. Measures for which statements on validity are not available should be used with extreme caution in evaluation processes.

Standardisation

There should ideally be sufficient data on a measure to be used as a reference system for the classification of the measured values; we require a uniform measurement scale for representation and comparison of empirically gathered values.

Standardisation may be achieved if sufficient measured values are available to determine their frequency distribution.

In the present state of software engineering, it is fair to say that standardisation is uncommon; in any case because, as we have seen, there is a strongly subjective element in the transformation of measured results to a judgement scale, standardisation is not always possible. We should therefore regard it as progress if we can obtain statements on either practical suitability for a specific domain or on empirically based suggestions as to probably useful standard scales.

Comparability

A measure is comparable if there are other measures that claim to measure the same characteristic. However, if such measures give widely different results when used for estimation, one would need to know a great deal about the underlying assumptions before one would know which one to choose. Such measures would by definition have a low degree of comparability. Even if they appear to give the same answer, some care is needed in case they are really the *same* measure expressed in a different way.

Nevertheless such correlations are a valuable means of comparing measures and ensuring that new measuring methods are truly valid. Mutual reliability checks can also be carried out.

Economy

A measure is economical if the determination and evaluation of measured values involves low cost in comparison with the benefit gained. The following may be of decisive importance:

- the number of measured values to be obtained;
- the number and difficulty of the computational steps needed to obtain the results;
- the ease of interpretation;
- the availability (and cost) of automation compared to the difficulty of manual calculation.

Usefulness

Usefulness indicates the extent to which a measure satisfies a practical need when it is used to quantify a particular characteristic. This depends on the importance of the characteristic to be measured, for the particular installation, and inversely on the number of other measures able to provide the same information. By way of warning, Drake (1982) indicates that many software characteristics can be measured very easily, even though there is no discernible need for the measured results. Perhaps, then, we are justified in saying that the easier it is to determine a measure, the sooner the user should question its usefulness.

6.2 VALIDATION PROCEDURES

Most software quality measures published to date describe relationships between characteristics (or attributes) and indicators without actually proving that they are valid. It is therefore not always clear whether a given measure really measures the characteristic which it claims to measure; this is particularly so where a measure is used in a new application.

We need therefore to look more deeply at validity. After that we will offer some guidelines, in the form of questions. If most of the answers are positive for a particular measure, then that measure appears to be valid. There will of course be 'degrees' of validity, though we indicate some questions which need to be answered positively.

These guidelines do not really save the software engineer from the work associated with proving validity – some apparently simple questions may require days or even weeks of effort to answer properly.

6.2.1 Validity

Content Validity

A measure only possesses 'content validity' to the extent that its content adequately represents the quality characteristic to be measured. When testing this facet of validity, there are two questions to be considered:

- Do the selected indicators actually allow one to infer that the quality characteristic is present?
- Do the selected indicators constitute a representative sample of all possible indicators of the given quality characteristic?

Except in the simplest cases, it is not possible for the average software engineer to assess the content validity by himself. Analysis must therefore be done by means of the estimation procedures described below.

These 'rating methods' need to be performed by experts: they are not entirely objective and the subjective preferences of the experts should be considered. There are four different types of rating:

Individual: this is when the degree of validity is classified by a single expert.

Collective: several experts together decide which value on the scale is to be assigned to the validity of a measure; the decision may be a compromise.

Average: this too involves a group of experts, but they perform their judgement individually. Subsequently, the various values obtained are averaged to an overall validity rating.

Multi-level (Delphi Method): this is an attempt to get the best judgement from a group of experts. To avoid social consent pressures, the experts do not need to meet personally. The distribution of the individual ratings (including its median, lower quartile, upper quartile, etc) is determined centrally. The experts are given this information and carry out a further (second level) individual rating.

This process (which may be repeated several times if necessary) usually leads to a convergence of the ratings, so that it is possible to determine the overall validity degree of the method being rated. The advantages are that even though the experts work on their own, the other judgements provide a stimulating, or perhaps correcting, influence: this has to be weighed against the effort required to carry out the method.

It can be a problem for the potential user of a method to find out whether a measure is considered valid. He is often reliant on the statements of the originator of the measure, unless there has been any subsequent discussion of the measure in available literature. This is one reason why we believe that our current work in opening up this area to a wider audience, publishing details of measures and their validity, will be valuable.

Empirical Validity

Determination of the 'empirical validity' requires criteria against which the measure can be compared. These may be either external or internal.

To determine *external validity,* the measured results are correlated with the values of an 'external criterion', which must represent or reflect the characteristic to be measured either directly or indirectly. There may be software where certain values have already been established. The measure has to be applied to this software and the measured values have to be compared with the given values.

For complexity, the number of lines of code is often taken as an external criterion against which individual complexity measures can be compared. High correlations have indeed been found, between some complexity measures and lines of code when used on PL/1 modules, as described in *Software quality: measurement and evaluation* (Christ et al, 1984). Having carried out such a correlation, however, it is tempting to assume that the LOC (lines of code) measure is sufficient and that one does not need the other measures which are much more difficult to calculate.

For the determination of *internal validity,* the measure is examined to see whether the results correlate with the values of other measures accepted as valid for the same quality characteristic. The result of this comparison can be represented by a 'validity coefficient'. This procedure assumes that measures already exist which measure the same characteristic and that these measures are valid (with respect to content or construct) or possess a high validity coefficient with respect to an external criterion.

The correlation coefficient can take values between zero and one. Usually the correlation coefficient is taken as follows:

0.0 to 0.4 – low correlation
0.4 to 0.7 – mean correlation
0.7 to 0.99 – high correlation
1.00 – total correlation

Construct Validity

The importance of construct validation lies in proving theoretically what the measure to be considered really measures. This requires more effort than the other two types of validation, as a number of analyses will have to be carried out on different perspectives, eg changing the relationships between the indicators, excluding some indicators or adding others. In general, construct validity has to be tested by correlation and factor analysis methods.

In testing, we are trying to find out whether the selection of

Indicators	Modularity (factor 1)	(factor 2)	(factor *n*)
Modules	0.69	0.07	0.18
Functions	0.63	0.10	0.25
Interfaces	0.56	0.17	0.42
Call structure	0.44	0.12	0.23
Local constants	0.19	0.56	0.43
Decision points	0.03	0.12	0.27
Local variables	0.01	0.19	0.09
Prop*n* of variance:	14.50	7.10	6.30
Cumulative prop*n*:	14.50	21.60	27.90

Table 6.1 Factor Analysis of 'Flexibility'

indicators is suitable for measuring the quality characteristic to be investigated and whether one could still get useful results with a smaller number of indicators. Further information will be found in many statistics text books.

For validating a construct one has to find all the possible indicators which could have an influence on the quality characteristic to be measured. The relevance of these indicators must then be determined by expert rating as discussed above. Then factor analysis can be performed to analyse all the relevance judgements. From this one gets a 'rank order' of the relevance of all the indicators. One can finally conclude how far each indicator determines a particular quality characteristic and thus decide the relative importance of the indicators and of the factors to which they belong.

Table 6.1 shows the result of a factor analysis for determining relevant factors of the quality characteristic 'flexibility'.

From this result we conclude that the first five indicators are relevant for this quality characteristic because each indicator has a factor loading of more than 0.40 on at least one factor. The first four indicators are all related to modularity (factor 1) and the proportion of variance indicates that the construct is determined to 14.5% by these four indicators.

So a measure which contains the first four indicators and which adequately considers their relevance (as expressed by the factor loadings) by suitable weightings would be construct valid. In this example the validity refers to modularity which seems to be a most important factor of flexibility.

There are further multivariate methods which could be used for testing construct validity, such as cluster analysis and multidimensional scaling (Overall and Klett 1972). These are not discussed here.

6.2.2 Validation of Software Quality Measures

To enable software developers to use measures for quality evaluation, objective and reliable statements on their validity would be very helpful. We have therefore developed a checklist which can be used when attempting to validate measures. The questions on this checklist will be found under six categories referring to:

- the quality characteristic to be measured;

- the indicators to be used:
  - selection;
  - weighting;
  - values;
- the type of measuring results;
- practical experience in the use of the measure.

Definition of the Quality Characteristic

Before investigating the validity of a measure, the definition of the characteristic to which it applies must be studied, especially the following aspects:

- Does there exist a satisfactory definition of the quality characteristic?
- Is the quality characteristic clearly distinguished from others?
- Is it possible (or rather perhaps are there any obvious ways) to determine the value of the quality characteristic?

Definition and Selection of Indicators

The use of appropriate indicators (eg product properties, economic values) is clearly crucial. The following questions should therefore be answered:

- Are definitions of the indicators available?
- Is it reasonable that these indicators should have values that can be used in quantitative or qualitative evaluation?
- Should the indicators be estimated or measured?
- Is the selection of indicators based on:
  - the experience of the developer of the measure;
  - sound empirical findings;
  - theoretically derived (but proven) hypotheses;
  - derivation from other measures;
  - some other source?

- Are the selected indicators relevant to the quality characteristic under examination?
- Do the selected indicators appear to be reliable?
- Is the number of indicators necessary and sufficient?
    - are essential indicators missing?
    - are there redundant indicators?

If any of the last three questions has to be answered in the negative, it will be necessary to stop the validation process at this point with the conclusion that the measure is not valid.

Connection and Weighting of Indicators

When defining a measure, one needs to be sure that the mathematical operators, weighting factors and constants are valid. Three problems are relevant:

- Are the indicators meaningfully connected?
- Is there a weighting of indicators by factors?
- If so, is their selection based soundly?

Values of Indicators

The assessors of the measure will want to know whether the measure is universal or restricted to a specific type of software. It will help them to know the values which have been found for various indicators in earlier use. They should find the answers to the following questions:

- Is there any statement as to the possible values which an indicator might take?
- Is the range of values restricted?
- Does one get completely different measuring results when indicators take different values? (This may happen when one indicator has, in previous testing always been in a restricted range, and suddenly takes a much higher value.)
- Does the weighting given to indicators reflect the assessors' view on the importance of these indicators?

Measuring Results

We have already discussed (in Chapter 2.4) the sort of scales which may be used and when they are appropriate. The following aspects are to be investigated:

- Which type of scale is used; nominal, ordinal interval or ratio?
- Is the type of scale appropriate?
- Are the scale values meaningful?
- Do the measuring results allow qualitative comparisons?
- Are the measured values realistic? In other words do different results represent corresponding differences of quality?
- Are there any statements on the type or significance level of the validity coefficient available?
- Is the measuring process defined clearly and described in such a manner that it can be followed?
- Are any tools available for performing measurement? Such instrumentation could be of great value if there is much measuring to be done or if the process is complicated.

The last two questions have less to do with validity than with economy and usability, but have been included for completeness.

Experience in the Use of a Measure

It may seem unkind to say so, but it appears that developers are always sure of the validity of their own measures. It is always helpful to know that it has been used by other people, and also the circumstances in which it has been used.

- Are experiences with the measure documented and available?
- Are experiences of persons other than the developer available?
- In what 'framework' has the measure been tested:
  - in field tests organised by the developer;
  - in laboratory experiments with students;
  - in 'industrial' (real world) software development?

- Has the measure been compared with other measures? What statements are available regarding its content, empirical and construct validity?

The results of validation procedures should be documented. It is hoped that the checklist given will provide a useful guideline. It may not be complete, but it will provide a validator with systematic support for testing the validity of a software quality measure.

7 Conclusions

CONCEPT FORMATION AND QUALITY MODELS

It is necessary to have a model of quality characteristics as a framework to hold the attributes and indicators which can be measured at levels of greater detail. When one starts this process of decomposition, it is sometimes hard to know where to stop. We believe that a framework like the one which we have described (in Chapter 3) will be of benefit to data processing managers and software engineers, whether their responsibility for quality is direct or indirect.

It would clearly be easier to discuss this subject if the concepts used were standard. This will not come about until people have themselves considered more fully what quality means to them.

At the company and individual level therefore, it is important that everyone should consider their own quality requirements and decide which characteristics are important. If companies can go further and specify these characteristics in terms of effort and cost attributes (for management) or quality attributes related to product properties (for practitioners), this will be very valuable, and could lead eventually to much wider sharing of this information for the benefit of the DP community as a whole.

We would like to see a wider pooling of knowledge. This might come about through working parties set up by such organisations as the British Computer Society, training courses in quality (which are now being organised), user groups or less formal gatherings. First however there must be knowledge to share, so people must try out the sort of measures described in outline in this book. We would therefore hope that research organisations and academic researchers will continue to develop measures and make sure that they are tried out on real problems, not just on small local software.

There are two sides to this on-going research: firstly, we want to have measures which give a proper evaluation when applied after the software has been written; secondly, we need to apply ourselves more seriously to the problems of prediction. It would clearly be of benefit for producers of software to know that the properties they build into their software will lead to 'good' quality in the end-product. The point of being able to measure the result against the predicted outcome is that this gives greater confidence that the desired quality really has been achieved.

THE QUALITY OF DESIGN METHODOLOGIES

This leads us then to consider the place of design methodologies. If these are good, they will ensure the production of better software. This is why we want to develop further the approach to selecting methodologies which was outlined in Chapter 5. In its present form, this approach requires that the scope and rating of the methodology should be set out for each time of use. This is obviously wasteful and we can therefore envisage building up a store of this information, with additional data about the experience of existing users.

Work on developing the questionnaire in the context of requirements definition methodologies has already been undertaken. A pilot study at the London School of Economics, under the guidance of Dr R Stamper, has looked at eight leading methodologies (Law, 1984). We now need to carry out a similar evaluation in a data processing installation, in order to be sure that the method is applicable in a commercial or industrial environment.

Software Quality Measures

We believe that most effort should be directed towards measures which contribute to reliability, maintainability and usability.

For *reliability,* as we have seen (Section 3.2.5) the Musa 'Execution Time Model' has some promise. We would therefore like to see controlled use of this in software producing organisations.

In *maintainability* (Section 3.3.1) we believe that the multiplicity of complexity measures is likely to cause bewilderment; there seems to be little advantage in developing new measures unless the existing ones have been tried and proved to be inadequate. We believe that as a simple pragmatic measure, the number of lines of code should be counted and used as an initial indicator of complexity; ratios of lines of code to effort and to error rates and other product properties might be calculated in the production environment in order to develop local standards (which could later form the basis for a wider survey).

Usability (Section 3.2.1) is crucial to all software, but so far it has not been possible to find measures which are universally applicable. Even those surveys of relevant characteristics such as those conducted by Dzida et al, 1978 are now out of date and not necessarily representative of today's user environment. Without an up-to-date factor analysis involving a large group of users, we are left with practical advice which may be based on biased personal experience rather than the needs of real users.

We would also wish to find more evidence of proper *validation* of those measures which are proposed for these areas and for all the other characteristics discussed in this report. We believe that the guidelines (Section 6.2) can provide a systematic basis for sound validation.

We are quite sure that the brief survey of multidimensional methods will be of value to anyone who attempts overall validation of software quality. The more complex methods will be of value to those who can be reasonably sure of the weighting factor values which they assign to the various characteristics and attributes.

Appendix 1

Summary of Measures

The purpose of this appendix is to give some additional guidance which will help the reader to decide whether it is worth taking an interest further, by giving a brief description and assessment and reference to the original sources. It is recommended that this is taken as a simplified guide and not as a compendium of firm recommendations. The measures are given in the same sequence that they appear in Table 3.1, that is in the order of the primary characteristics discussed in Chapter 3.

1 USABILITY

1.1 Flesch-Kincaid Readability Index (see Section 3.2.1)

Source: Kincaid JP, Aagard JA, O'Hara JW, Cottrell LK, Computer readability editing system, *IEEE transactions on professional communication,* 1981, vol PC-24 no 1, pp 38-41

This index is a syllable-based readability formula which aims at predicting and controlling the level of difficulty of prose text material. It is simple to calculate manually and computer-assisted calculation is also possible. This index is used in the US DoD as a Standard (MIL-M-38784A) for the development of user manuals and training material.

1.2 Fog Index

Source: Gunning R, *The technique of clear writing,* McGraw-Hill, 1968 (revised edition)

The Fog Index is proposed as a measure for the reading ease level of software documents written in English. It measures the 'fogginess' of the text. The lower the index, the less complex the text is. It should be emphasised that it is better regarded (even by the author) as a warning rather than as a writing formula. It is relatively easy to compute manually but computer programs have been written.

1.3 Keystroke-level Model

Source: Card SK, Moran TP, Newell A, The keystroke-level model for user performance time with interactive systems, *CACM,* 1980, vol 23, no 7, pp 396-409

This measure attempts to make predictions on the total time that it will take for a user to carry out a given task, based on past execution performance. It might therefore be possible to compare alternative methods of carrying out a particular task. There is no evidence yet that it has been used outside the research environment.

1.4 Measure of User Friendliness

Source: Maier HH, Die Prüfung des Software-Qualitätsmerkmals Benutzungsfreundlichkeit, *QZ Management der Qualitätssicherung,* 1983, 28, vol 1

The author has attempted to link the time taken for the operation and user satisfaction. This is to get round the observed effect that more expert users prefer to have some challenge in their use of interactive systems. This measure therefore has an advantage over any simple statistics that only take note of time taken (eg Keystroke-level Model above). The allocation of scores to the elementary items on the checklist is bound to be subjective.

2 INTEGRITY

2.1 Integrity Metrics

Source: Svanks MI, Integrity analysis: a methodology for EDP audit and data quality control, *(Thesis) TR131,* Computer Science Research Group, University of Toronto, July 1981

The metrics are introduced as part of a methodology called 'integrity analysis' which examines a database with the objectives of identifying and confirming errors, determining other indicators of deficiencies and providing a quality control mechanism for data. It is likely that computation would be difficult, the integrity measure does, however, appear to be objective.

3 EFFICIENCY
None (see text)

4 CORRECTNESS
(Section 3.2.4)

4.1 Error Prediction Measure

Source: Ottenstein LM, Quantitative estimates of debugging requirements, *IEEE transactions on software engineering,* 1979, vol SE-5, no 5, pp 504-514;

Ottenstein LM, Predicting the number of errors using software science, *Proceedings of the ACM annual conference,* 1981, pp 157-167

Ottenstein predicts the number of errors using Halstead's software science parameters. Two totals are predicted, the number of errors that will be found during the validation phase, and the number to be found during the whole development process. It is suggested that this sort of measure may be valid in a stable environment and statistics need therefore to be gathered for each installation wishing to make use of it. The constants may need to be adjusted.

4.2 Model of Defect Removal

Source: Remus H, Zilles S, Prediction and management of program quality, *Proceedings of the fourth international conference on software engineering,* 1979, pp 341-350

The model of the defect removal process can be used to estimate the effectiveness of the process as a whole and the number of defects which remain in software at any time (eg at the date of delivery to the customer). The model is based on two basic assumptions:

- that each piece of software starts with a set of original defects, the number of which depends largely on the length of the programs;

- that there is a sequence of defect removal steps in which each defect is discovered and corrected. The model uses a formula to predict how many errors will be discovered at each stage. In order to use this, one needs up-to-date statistics for current products, eg about the efficiency of various defect removal techniques. Without such information, one could use other people's data and refine it later in the light of one's own experience.

4.3 Pimont and Rault's Testing Measure

Source: Pimont S, Rault JC, A software reliability assessment based on a structural and behavioural analysis of programs, *Proceedings of the second international conference on software engineering,* 1976, pp 486-491

This test measure is based on observation of a specific category of paths in structured Fortran programs. It is probably usable with other programming languages since the analysis can be done on the flowchart. The measure attempts to determine how exhaustively the program has been tested by comparing test paths with theoretically possible paths.

5 RELIABILITY (Section 3.2.5)

5.1 Complexity Measure based on Selection and Nesting

Source: Gong H, Schmidt M, A complexity measure based on selection and nesting, submitted for publication to ACM Sigmetrics, St Augustin, FRG

This extends McCabe's Cyclomatic Number (5.5 below) to take account of the degree of nesting of the selection nodes of the control graph.

5.2 Gilb's Logical Complexity Measure

Source: Gilb T, *Software metrics,* Winthrop Publishers, 1977

This is a simple to apply measure which produces a measure of the complexity of a program by counting the number of binary decision instructions. It is also possible to determine the relative logical complexity by finding the ratio of decision instructions to the total number of instructions. It is then possible to relate complexity to other software characteristics like cost, reliability and maintainability.

5.3 Knot Count Complexity Measure

Source: Woodward MR, Hennell MA, Hedley D, A measure of control flow complexity in program text, *IEEE transactions on software engineering,* 1979, vol SE-5, no 1, pp 45-50

This measure can be used only on Fortran programs to determine their complexity. Well-structured programs show few 'knots', which are a sign of over complicated control flow. The authors have an automatic tool for counting knots.

5.4 Maximal Intersection Number

Source: Chen ET, Program complexity and programmer productivity, *IEEE transactions on software engineering,* 1978, vol SE-4, no 3, pp 187-194

This measure can be used on structured program flowcharts to determine the complexity of the program flow. The author has applied the procedure to programs generated by different groups of programmers and claims a functional relationship between program complexity and programmer productivity.

5.5 Interval Complexity Measure

Source: Myers GJ, An extension to the cyclomatic measure of program complexity, *ACM SIGPLAN notices,* 1977, vol 12, no 10, pp 61-64

This is another extension to McCabe's Cyclomatic Number. In this case Myers considers the number of conditions as well as the number of decision statements.

5.6 Thayer's Logic Complexity Measure

Source: Thayer TA, Lipow M, Nelson EC, *Software reliability study TRW-SS-76-03,* IEEE Computer Society, 1977

Logic complexity is related to source code statements of logic relationships, primarily branching decisions, but including loop and IF-nesting level parameters. The measure takes account of these factors in measuring complexity, which can be used as an indicator of reliability.

5.7 2-tuple Complexity Measure

Source: Hansen WJ, Measurement of program complexity by the pair (cyclomatic number, operator count), *ACM SIGPLAN notices,* April 1978, pp 29-33

Hansen proposes to measure complexity with 'lexicographically ordered 2-tuples' consisting of the cyclomatic number and the number of operators, which is a measure of expression complexity.

5.8 Execution Time Measure

Source: Musa JD, The measurement and management of software reliability, *Proceedings of the IEEE,* 1980, vol 68, no 9, pp 1131-1143

This measure is discussed in the text. Musa has derived a measure relating to failures experienced, present mean time to failure (MTTF), cumulative execution time, MTTF objective, failures to be experienced and the execution and calendar time needed to meet the objective. The resultant reliability appears (in testing of 16 software systems) to be valid.

5.9 Nelson's Reliability Measure

Source: Nelson EC, A statistical basis for software reliability assessment, *TRW software series* TRW-SS-73-03, IEEE, June 1977

Reliability may be measured by considering all the possible 'tests' of a program and the number for which runs of the program construct incorrect function values. The author appears to use relatively simple concepts but no information is available about reliability or validity.

5.10 Numerical Reliability Index

Source: Hecht H, Measurement, estimation and prediction of software reliability, *Software engineering techniques,* Infotech, 1977

This measure is similar to the last. For batch processing and on-line systems dealing with discrete operations, the ratio of successful to total trials over a period is a good indicator of reliability. For real-time systems dealing with continuous streams of data, the mean time between failures (MTBF) is more significant. It should be noted that such measures in this simple form are only meaningful in a particular environment (in other words they are good enough for an installation where all programs are comparable, but not for wider use unless normalised).

5.11 Probabilistic Measure of Reliability

Source: Schick GJ, Wolverton RW, An analysis of competing software reliability models, *IEEE transactions on software engineering,* 1978, vol SE-4, no 2, pp 104-120

The measure makes the assumption that, given a certain number of initial errors and the interval between error discovery, the remaining error time distribution can be calculated. It would need to be validated in a new environment, where for example different types of errors might lead to different results.

5.12 Littlewood's Measure of Availability

Source: Littlewood B, How to measure software reliability and how not to... *Proceedings of the third international conference on software engineering,* IEEE, 1978, pp 37-45

The author calculates the availability as the ratio of MTTF to total time (MTTF + MTTR [mean time to repair]). The percentage of the possible running time that the system is available for normal operation is determined; this is 'interval' availability (as distinct from 'point' availability which is the probability that the system will be able to operate at a given time). The measure appears simple but values for MTTF and MTTR will not necessarily be easy to predict.

6 MAINTAINABILITY (Section 3.3.1)

6.1 De Young/Kampen's Readability Measure

Source: De Young GE, Kampen GR, Program factors as

predictors of program readability, *Proceedings of the computer software and applications conference,* IEEE, 1979, pp 668-673

This measure determines the readability of programs using three 'predictors'. It is said to be particularly suitable for medium sized or larger programs written in block-structured languages (eg PL/1, Pascal, Algol). It is based on a survey of a large number of *student* programs where the results were subjected to a multiple regression process to determine their significance. The predictors are the number of statement lines, the average length of variables and the total number of program branches. An additional variable, well-structured control flow, was later added, after examination of a number of other factors.

6.2 Gordon's Program Clarity Measure

Source: Gordon RD, A qualitative justification for a measure of program clarity, *IEEE transactions on software engineering,* 1979, vol SE-5, no 2, pp 121-128

Gordon RD, Measuring Improvements in program clarity, *IEEE transactions on software engineering,* 1979, vol SE-5, no 2, pp 79-90

Gordon's Measure is similar to Halstead's Effort Measure. Both authors agree that the major determining factor is the mental effort required to understand the program. The mental effort is entirely determined by the structural characteristics of the program code, and this could well be one of the weaknesses of this method. It would however be worth the attempt to calibrate such methods in real organisations.

6.3 Joergensen's Readability Measure

Source: Joergensen AH, A methodology for measuring the readability and modifiability of programs, *BIT,* 1980, vol 20, pp 394-405

The measure is based on a formula derived from a subjective evaluation of the readability of 48 application programs (written in Algol-60). The evaluation was carried out by a group of data processing experts and the results subjected to a linear regression analysis. A large number of variables were involved, which would make manual calculation difficult. The variables could however be computer produced though no actual instrumentation is reported to be available.

6.4 Halstead's Effort Measure E

> *Source:* Halstead MH, *Elements of software science,* Elsevier, 1977

Software science, of which this measure forms part, is based on counts of operators and operands of a program from which statements on program volume and level, program difficulty, language level, etc, can be derived. The effort is given by the program volume and difficulty. There has been a great deal of discussion of these measures and it is now established (we believe) that at best the measure can only be valid for reasonably stable programming environments and would require testing and/or adjusting before it could be transported. Nevertheless, it would make a good starting point when looking for measures in this area.

6.5 McCabe's Cyclomatic Number

> *Source:* McCabe TJ. A complexity measure, *IEEE transactions on software engineering,* 1976, vol SE-2, no 4, pp 308-320

McCabe's cyclomatic number has been much discussed in literature (and further developed). It is based on graph theory – the measure counts (or estimates) the number of linearly independent paths through the program. Complexity is here determined entirely by the control flow, irrespective of the program length. The formula is reasonably easy to use for manual calculations.

6.6 McClure's Complexity Measure

> *Source:* McClure CL, A model for program complexity analysis, *Proceedings of the third international conference on software engineering, IEEE, 1978, pp 149-157*

This measure attempts to determine the complexity of the control variables, which is governed by the number of modules and their 'call' relationship. The program complexity is the sum of module complexities. One advantage of the measure is that it can be used during the design stage as a guide to the simplification of the design.

6.7 Oviedo's Complexity Measure

Source: Oviedo EI, Control flow, data flow and program complexity, *Proceedings of the computer software and applications conference,* IEEE, 1980, pp 146-152

Oviedo has attempted to analyse and measure control flow and data flow. It appears to be consistent with other measures and subjective assessment.

6.8 Yin and Winchester's Measure for Software Design Quality

Sources: Yin BH, Winchester JW, The establishment and use of measures to evaluate the quality of software designs, *ACM software engineering notes,* 1978, vol 3, no 5, pp 45-52

Yin BH, Software design testability analysis, *Proceedings of the computer software and applications conference,* IEEE, 1980, pp 729-734

This measure can be used on any hierarchical tree-structure design. The complexity is determined by recording all modules and the connections existing between them. Instrumentation has been developed by the authors to compute the values for complexity.

6.9 Zolnowski and Simmons' Complexity Measure

Source: Zolnowski JM, Simmons DB, A complexity measure applied to Fortran, *Proceedings of the computer software and applictions conference,* IEEE, 1977, pp 133-141

This measure considers the instruction mix, the data references, interaction and interconnection and finally the structure and control flow. Evaluation of these leads to an overall complexity measure. If the authors are right, it means that the complexity measures that are simple and easy to calculate are likely to be inadequate, because they ignore important factors.

6.10 Logical Stability Measure

Source: Yau SS, Collofello JS, Some stability measures for software maintenance, *Proceedings of the computer software and applications conference,* IEEE, 1979, pp 674-679

The stability measure is based on recording the 'ripple effects' resulting from a program modification. The ripple effects are a measure of the number of modules affected. It is necessary to use another complexity measure to determine the complexity of the individual modules.

6.11 Gilb's Structural Complexity Measure

Source: Gilb T, *Software metrics,* Winthrop Publishers, 1977

The author has formulated two complexity measures concerned with relationships between modules. It is necessary to count the number of modules and the number of connections between them. He ignores (in this measure) the complexity within the module and complications to do with the control flow. It would be a simple measure to apply.

6.12 Keutgen's Modularity Metric

Source: Keutgen H, Eine Metric zur Bewertung des Modularisierung, *Tagungsbund G1-11,* Bauer W, ed, Springer Verlag, 1981, pp 191-199

This measure is based on a four-layer modularisation model. The layers, which can themselves be subdivided if necessary, are:

- control modules;
- problem-orientated modules;
- management modules for abstract data types;
- realisation modules for abstract data types.

Having assumed an 'onion shape' (whereby the number of modules starts small, increases rapidly and then either decreases slightly or remains constant), the measure looks for deviations from this shape which might show up deficiencies. Manual calculation of large systems would require considerable effort; a calculating instrument is being developed

6.13 Module Independence Measure

Source: Myers GJ, *Software reliability: principles and practices,*

Wiley Interscience Publications, 1976

The author offers a measure of modularity, based on the 'internal strength' of the modules and the number of 'intermodular couplings'.

6.14 Mohanty and Adamowicz's Test Measures

Source: Mohanty SN, Adamowicz M, Proposed measures for the evaluation of software; *Proceedings of the symposium on computer software engineering,* Microwave Research Institute of the Polytechnic Institute of New York, 1976, pp 485-497

The authors have developed their measures on the logical structure. Static measures are first made to determine the testability of any path, and these are then supplemented with dynamic determination of test effectiveness. Whereas the former could be carried out manually, the latter requires information about the frequency of execution of given paths.

6.15 Test Effort Measure

Source: Paige M, A metric for software test planning, *Proceedings of the computer software and applications conference,* IEEE, 1980, pp 499-504

The author attempts to measure test effort by means of two interacting individual measures. The measure NK, nesting level index, reflects the classification depth of the decision instructions. This serves as an indicator of the number of tests needed. This is combined with Halstead's Measure E, the warnings for which also apply here.

6.16 Test Effectiveness Metrics

Source: Woodward MR, Hedley D, Hennell MA, Experience with path analysis and testing programs. *IEEE transactions on software engineering,* 1980, vol SE-6, no 3, pp 278-286

The authors have devised tests (and instrumentation) to measure the extent to which possible program paths have been covered, because this determines the test effectiveness to a considerable degree. The lowest level is a single LCSAJ (linear code sequence and jumps), ie an instruction sequence at the end of which there is a jump in the control flow. Test paths are made by combining these. It would be very difficult to do this manually in a program of any size.

6.17 Independence Metric

Source: Yin BH, Software design testability analysis, *Proceedings of the computer software and applications conference,* IEEE, 1980, pp 729-734

This measure assumes the existence of so-called 'independent areas' within a software system, that is areas which possess an input module and can only be reached through this module. The author believes that increasing the number (by reducing the size) of the independent areas will lead to improvements in testability.

7 ADAPTABILITY
None (see under Maintainability)

8 EXPANDABILITY
(Section 3.3.3)

8.1 Measure of Extensibility

Source: Maekawa M, Extensibility and adaptability of distributed computing systems, *Proceedings of the computer software and applications conference,* IEEE, 1980, pp 313-319

The author defines this measure in terms of interconnections and proposes the optimal interconnection of processing components. The measure indicates how the ratio of cost to performance behaves when the system grows. System performance, in terms of the number of components and the processing power of a single component, have to be discovered first.

9 INTEROPERABILITY
None (see under Maintainability)

10 RESUSABILITY
None (See text)

11 PORTABILITY
(Section 3.4.1)

11.1 Portability Measure

Source: Gilb T, *Software metrics, Winthrop Publishers, 1977*

Used after the event, this portability measure will show the ease of conversion of a system from one environment to another in terms of resources used. The author suggests such portability may be predicted by extrapolation from the ease of converting a subsystem; this would of course assume a linear progression as the size of the software is increased. This is in line with the discovery that complexity (and hence the number of errors), may be predicted by considering the number of lines of code.

Appendix 2

Bibliography

Abbott J, *Software test aids,* DP circle report, NCC, 1985

Abbott J, *Software validation: techniques and methods,* DP circle report, NCC, 1984

André et al, *Programming techniques,* Final report to CEC, GMD, IRIA, NCC, 1980

Belady LA, Leavenworth B, *Program modifiability,* IBM, 1980

Belady LA, Lehman MM, A model of large program development, *IBM systems journal,* 1976, vol 15, no 3, pp 225-252

Boehm BW et al, *Characteristics of software quality,* TRW series of software technology, 1978, vol 1

Card SK, Moran TP, Newell A, The keystroke-level model for user performance time with interactive systems, *CACM,* 1980, vol 23, no 7, pp 396-409

Chen ET, Program complexity and programmer productivity, *IEEE transactions on software engineering,* 1978, vol SE-4, no 3, pp 187-194

Christ ML et al, *Software quality: measurement and evaluation,* SDSS-MQ final report, NCC, 1984

De Young GE, Kampen GR, Program factors as predictors of program readability, *Proceedings of the computer software and applications conference,* IEEE, 1979, pp 668-673

Department of Industry, *Ada-based system development methodology,* Study report, DTI, 1981

Drake D, ed, Proposal: software quality research. Focus maintainability, *ACM software engineering notes,* 1982, vol 7, no 1, pp 13-20

Dunn R, Ullman R, *Quality assurance for computer software,* McGraw-Hill, 1982

Dzida W, Herda S, Itzfeldt WD, *Factors of user-perceived quality of interactive systems,* GMD, Report no 40, 1978

Feuer AR, Fowlkes EB, Relating computer program reliability to software measures, *Proceedings of the national computer conference,* IEEE, 1979, pp 1003-1012

Feuer AR, Fowlkes EB, Some results from an empirical study of computer software, *Proceedings of the fourth international conference on software engineering,* IEEE, 1979, pp 351-355

Freeman P, Wasserman AI, *Software development methodologies and Ada: concepts and requirements,* Ada Joint Program Office, 1982

Freund RA, Definitions and basic quality concepts, *Journal of quality technology,* 1985, vol 17, no 1

Funami Y, Halstead MH, *A software physics analysis of Akiyama's debugging data,* Lafayette, 1975

Gilb T, *Design by objectives,* North-Holland, 1987

Gilb T, *Software metrics,* Winthrop Publishers, 1977

Gong H, Schmidt M, *A complexity measure based on selection and nesting,* Submitted for publication to ACM Sigmetrics

Gordon RD, A qualitative justification for a measure of program clarity, *IEEE transactions on software engineering,* 1979, vol SE-5, no 2, 121-128

Gordon RD, Measuring improvements in program clarity, *IEEE transactions on software engineering,* 1979, vol SE-5, no 2, pp 79-90

Gunning R, *The technique of clear writing* (revised edition), McGraw-Hill, 1968

Halstead MH, *Elements of software science,* Elsevier, 1977

Hamer PG, Frewin GD, MH Halstead's software science — a critical examination, *Proceedings of the sixth international conference on software engineering, IEEE, 1982*

Hansen WJ, Measurement of program complexity by the pair (cyclomatic number, operator count), *ACM SIGPLAN notices,* April 1978, pp 29-33

Hecht H, Fault-tolerant software, *IEEE transactions on software,* 1979, vol R-28, no 3, pp 227-232

Hecht H, Measurement, estimation and prediction of software reliability, *Software engineering techniques,* Infotech, 1977

Hoecker H et al, *Comparative descriptions of software quality measures,* Technical paper from SDSS-MQ8, GMD, 1984

Iannino A et al, Criteria for software reliability model comparison, *ACM SIGSOFT software engineering notes,* 1983, vol 8, no 3, pp 12-16

Joergensen AH, A methodology for measuring the readability and modifiability of programs, *BIT,* 1980, vol 20, pp 394-405

Kaposi AA, Kitchenham B, The architecture of system quality, *Software engineering journal,* 1987, vol 2, no 1

Kaposi AA, Markusz Z, Objective metrics of structural complexity, *Designing for system complexity,* Pergamon Infotech state-of-the-art report, 1985

Kepner CH, Tregoe BB, *Entscheidungen vorbereiten und richtig treffen. Rationales Management: die neue Herausforderung,* Verlag Moderne Industrie, 1981

Keutgen H, Eine Metric zur Bewertung des Modularisierung, Bauer W, ed, *Tagungsbund G1-11,* 1981, pp 191-199

Kincaid JP, Aagard JA, O'Hara JW, Computer readability editing system, *IEEE transactions on professional communication,* 1981, vol PC-24, no 1, pp 38-41

Krten OJ, Levy DA, Software modelling for optimal field entry, *Proceedings of the annual reliability and maintainability symposium,* IEEE, 1980, pp 410-414

Law D, *Building quality models of software development aids,* Technical paper from SDSS-MQ5, NCC, 1983

Law D, *Criteria for comparing methodologies for defining system requirements,* Technical paper 1 from SDSS-RSUB5, NCC, 1984

Leveson NG, Software safety, *ACM software engineering notes,* 1982, vol 7, no 2, pp 21-24

Littlewood B, How to measure software reliability and how not to... *Proceedings of the third international conference on software engineering,* IEEE, 1978, pp 37-45

Littlewood B, Verrall JL, A Bayesian reliability growth model for computer software, *Journal of the Royal Statistical Society,* Series C, 1973, vol 22, no 3, pp 332-346

Littlewood B, Verrall JL, A Bayesian reliability model with a stochastically monotone failure rate, *IEEE transactions on reliability,* 1974, vol R-23, pp 108-114

Longworth G, *Designing for change,* Technical paper for SDSS-SD1, NCC, 1983

Maekawa M, Extensibility and adaptability of distributed computing systems, *Proceedings of the computer software and applications conference,* IEEE, 1980, pp 313-319

Maier HH, Die Prüfung des Software-Qualitätsmerkmals Benutzungsfreundlichkeit, *QZ Management der Qualitätssicherung,* 1983, vol 1, no 28

McCabe TJ, A complexity measure, *IEEE transactions on software engineering,* 1976, vol SE-2, no 4, pp 308-320

McCall JA, An assessment of current software metric research, *Proceedings EASCON80,* IEEE, 1980, 323-333

McCall JA, Richards PK, Walters GF, Concepts and definitions of software quality, *Factors in software quality,* NTIS, 1977, vol 1

McClure CL, A model for program complexity analysis, *Proceedings of the third international conference on software engineering,* IEEE, 1978, pp 149-157

Mohanty SN, Adamowicz M, Proposed measures for the evaluation of software, *Proceedings of the symposium on computer software engineering,* Microwave Research Institute of the Polytechnic Institute of New York, 1976, pp 485-497

Musa JD, A theory of software reliability and its applications, *IEEE transactions on software engineering,* 1975, vol SE-1, pp 312-327

Musa JD, Software reliability measurement, *Journal of systems and software,* 1980, no 1/3, pp 223-241

Musa JD, The measurement and management of software reliability, *Proceedings of the IEEE,* 1980, vol 68, no 9, pp 1131-1143

Musa JD, Validity of execution-time theory of software reliability *IEEE transaction on reliability,* 1979, vol R-28, no 3, pp 181-191

Myers GJ, An extension to the cyclomatic measure of program complexity, *ACM SIGPLAN notices,* 1977, vol 12, no 10, pp 61-64

Myers GJ, *Reliable software through composite design,* Petrocelli, 1975

Myers GJ, *Software reliability: principles and practices,* Wiley Interscience Publications, 1976

Nelson EC, *A statistical basis for software reliability assessment,* TRW software series TRW-SS-73-03, IEEE, June 1977

Ottenstein LM, Predicting numbers of errors using software science, *Proceedings of the ACM annual conference,* ACM, 1981, pp 157-167

Ottenstein LM, Quantitative estimates of debugging requirements, *IEEE transactions on software engineering,* IEEE, 1979, vol SE-5, no 5, pp 504-514

Overall JE, Klett CJ, *Applied multivariate analysis,* McGraw-Hill, 1972

Paige M, A metric for software test planning, *Proceedings of the computer software and applications conference,* IEEE, 1980, pp 499-504

Parnas DL, Designing software for ease of extension and contraction, *IEEE transactions on software engineering.* 1979, vol SE-5, p 128

Perlis A, Sayward F, Shaw M, *Software metrics: an analysis and evaluation,* MIT Press, 1981

Pimont S, Rault JC, A software reliability assessment based on a structural and behavioural analysis of programs, *Proceedings of the second international conference on software engineering, IEEE,* 1976, pp 486-491

Quality assurance and control, Final report of SDSS-QAC project, GMD and NCC, 1984

Remus H, Zilles, S, Prediction and management of program quality, *Proceedings of the fourth international conference on software engineering,* IEEE, 1979, pp 341-350

Rzevski G, A technique for fault-tolerant reliability assessment, *Proceedings of the sixth conference on advances in reliability technology,* IEEE, 1980

Schick GJ, Wolverton RW, An analysis of competing software reliability models, *IEEE transactions on software engineering,* 1978, vol SE-4, no 2, pp 104-120

Schmitz P et al, *Ein Kombinationsverfahren für Rangfolgeentscheidungen,* Schriftreihe des Rechenzentrums der Universitäat zu Köln, March 1975, vol 23

Sheppard SB et al, *Factors affecting programmer performance in a debugging task,* General Electric software management research, February 1979, vol TR-79-388100-5

Svanks MI, Integrity analysis: a methodology for EDP audit and data quality control, *(Thesis) TR131,* Computer Science Research Group, University of Toronto, July 1981

Thayer TA, Lipow M, Nelson EC, *Software reliability study TRW-SS-76-03* IEEE Computer Society, 1977

Watts RA, *Introducing interactive computing,* NCC Publications, 1984

Watts RA, *Use of quality models in evaluating software development aids,* SDSS technical paper, NCC, 1983

Whitty RW, Fenton NE, The axiomatic approach to system complexity, *Designing for system complexity,* Pergamon Infotech state-of-the-art report, 1985

Woodfield SN, Dunsmore HE, Shen VY, The effect of modularisation and comments on program comprehension, *Proceedings of the fifth international conference on software engineering,* IEEE, 1981, pp 215-223

Woodward MR, Hedley D, Hennell MA, Experience with path analysis and testing programs, *IEEE transactions on software engineering,* 1980, vol SE-6, no 6 pp 278-286

Woodward MR, Hennell MA, Hedley D, A measure of control flow complexity in program text, *IEEE transactions on software engineering,* 1979, vol SE-5, no 1, pp 45-50

Yau SS, Collofello JS, Some stability measures for software maintenance, *Proceedings of the computer software and applications conference,* IEEE, 1979, pp 674-679

Yin BH, Software design testability analysis, *Proceedings of the computer software and applications conference,* IEEE, 1980, pp 729-734

Yin BH, Winchester JW, The establishment and use of measures to evaluate the quality of software designs, *ACM software engineering notes,* 1978, vol 3, no 5, pp 45-52

Zolnowski JM, Simmons DB, A complexity measure applied to Fortran, *Proceedings of the computer software and applications conference,* IEEE, 1979, pp 674-679

Index